PERSONALITY PATHOLOGY

D1607854

PERSONALITY PATHOLOGY
Developmental Perspectives

Gilles Delisle

Translated from French by Dinah M. Ashcroft,
Lynne Rigaud, and Anne Kearns

KARNAC

First published in 2011 by
Karnac Books Ltd
118 Finchley Road
London NW3 5HT

British Library Cataloguing in Publication Data

A C.I.P. for this book is available from the British Library

ISBN-13: 978-1-85575-727-1

Typeset by Vikatan Publishing Solutions (P) Ltd., Chennai, India

www.karnacbooks.com

CONTENTS

ACKNOWLEDGMENTS

This book has been several years in the making. The fact that it has been completed, in spite of the hazards and obstacles of my professional and personal life, is due to the support, the presence, and the encouragement of a group of people, without whom the writing would have been too solitary an activity.

Firstly, I wish to thank Dinah M. Ashcroft and Lynne Rigaud who undertook the meticulous and difficult task of translating the original French text into English. Without their linguistic and clinical expertise, this project would never have seen the light of day.

Next, I must thank Jacqueline Bentley for rekindling interest in my work in the UK. The impetus for publishing this work in English came from the series of workshops that she organized in Swindon in 2008 and 2010.

Finally, I wish to express my deepest gratitude to Anne Kearns for her careful reading and correcting of the final draft and for her dedication to making this work intelligible to the English speaking reader.

AUTHOR BIOGRAPHY

Gilles Delisle, Ph.D., is a clinical psychologist and associate professor of clinical psychology at the University of Sherbrooke. He is the director of clinical training at the Centre d'Intégration Gestaltiste in Montreal, and a guest trainer at several training institutes abroad. He is a member of the International Society for the Study of Personality Disorders and of the International Neuropsychoanalysis Society. In 2010, he was appointed President of the State Advisory Council on Psychotherapy and was awarded the prestigious Noel-Mailloux Prize by the Quebec Order of Psychologists in recognition of lifetime achievement of scientific and professional excellence in clinical psychology.

INTRODUCTION

I trained as a clinical psychologist in the 1970s. Like all psychologists in Quebec, in the course of my studies I came across three major schools of thought in clinical psychology: psychoanalysis, behaviourism, and humanistic psychology. For all sorts of good and bad reasons of which I have written elsewhere (Delisle, 1999), I quickly felt a rapport with the existential-humanistic school and a bit later with Gestalt-therapy. My first training was in Montreal with Susan Saros, then in San Diego with Erving and Miriam Polster. During that decade I had the opportunity to work with Laura Perls, Isadore From, Jim Simkin and several others from the first generation of Gestaltists.

Now, a quarter of a century later, I still flex the "experiential muscles" that I developed as a result of my contact with those enthusiastic and exciting trainers. However, after the end of the 1980s, I found myself taking a different route in search of something that I felt was missing from my practice as a clinician. Gestalt-therapy had given me a way of being with another person in the here and now but it had not helped me to understand or even think about the lifelong journey of that person. Gestalt-therapy had made no secret that there was no developmental theory and therefore no theory of pathogenesis within its conceptual framework. From the standpoint of Gestalt epistemology there is no incongruence in that view, as I have attempted to show in *Object Relations in Gestalt-therapy*. By the end of the 1980s I had reached the conclusion that I could not be consistent as a practitioner and teacher if I continued to stick to the phenomenological approach outlined in Perls, Hefferline, and Goodman (1951), on whose theories I based my clinical work.

From this starting point I decided to revisit both the classical theories of personality disorder and the classifications of contemporary psychiatry. This was an attempt to reconcile the psychiatric classification of the *Diagnostic and Statistical Manual of Mental Disorders* (DSM) with the phenomenology of the contact-boundary as taught by Erving and Miriam Polster (Delisle, 1991).

Then after 1992, using material gathered from my seminars on theory and practice held in Paris and Montréal, I started to investigate some of the similarities between Perls's Gestalt theory of the Self and some of the post-Freudian developmental theories.

These attempts, though stimulating were not satisfactory: it still seemed to me that the Gestalt-therapy, that I was practising, an experiential presence with a scattering of often contradictory theories, lacked an integrated core structure. I wanted to avoid the oversimplification of eclecticism in favour of an integrative approach. This was the basis of my doctoral thesis, *Object Relations in Gestalt-therapy*, published in 1998. This work proposed integrating into the theory of Self a core structure, which allowed us to consider personality disorder without giving up the fundamental parameters of field theory.

If we are to start from this point we must consider that the fundamental etiological structure of personality disorder is multifaceted, that it is rooted in the developmental field and maintains itself by introducing specific distortions into the experiential field. From there on, it becomes theoretically useful and clinically essential to take account of the developmental field and the dynamics of its different issues.

Almost by accident, in 1998 I began some research for my theoretical and clinical teaching work that led me to the study of three great developmental axes: attachment, self-esteem, and eroticism. In 1997 I had been invited by the congress of the Order of Psychologists in Quebec to run a workshop on narcissistic issues in psychotherapy. Normally I would spend about 20 hours preparing for a six-hour workshop. But, after many days of reading, analysing session notes and case studies, I discovered with a mixture of naïve stupor and excitement, that I had stumbled into a world of theoretical and clinical knowledge, full of complex theories, woolly simplification, contradictory views, sometimes enlightening, sometimes suspect. ... In the course of the next five years I tried to sort out this material, test it clinically, organize and integrate it into the framework of the developmental theory of the Self that I had touched on in my thesis. I wanted to follow the rules of epistemology that I had adopted up to that time. From 1998, I had the opportunity to present this material to several hundreds of mental health professionals at a series of seminars and workshops that I had presented in Quebec and abroad on the topic of developmental issues.

This book is the outcome of this research. It is enriched by the discussions resulting from those seminars as well as by the practice of those who attended them. I do not claim to have reached a proper conclusion. Every year thousands of articles about each of the themes that we have touched on here are published in various professional or scientific reviews. There is a growing distance between the generalist's practice and our increasingly precise scientific knowledge.

However, no one can read everything and therefore it behoves us to ask ourselves the following questions. Is the most recent better than what came before? Is the measurable and demonstrable necessarily clinically interesting? Must what interests the clinician be measured and proved?

While theory and clinical research are becoming increasingly precise, innumerable socio-economic forces are pressing for a simplification in clinical practice. "Shrinks" are fashionable! They are everywhere: in the workplace, on television, on the radio. Their services are paid for by private or company insurance, provided that it is a "quick fix", not too expensive, and that we do not indulge in vague meanderings round "*mal de vivre*"!, dissatisfaction with life!

In short, the generalist today finds himself torn between two opposing forces. He seeks to practise from a secure base and to keep his knowledge up to date, while being aware that this in turn will give rise to an increasingly varied clinical practice, in which he deals with serious pathologies as well as working with patients requesting help in more ordinary situations. Whatever the profile of his practice the generalist has to be able to work with personality disorders and

understand how they arise. This essential competence enables him
to make informed clinical decisions.

So, the modest aim of this book is to be of use to the generalist in his daily practice. Of course it does not exempt anyone from
thinking and doing his own reading according to his interests and
particular queries.

The integrative structure which is the basis of this work is known
both as Relational Psychotherapy and as Object Relational Gestalt-
therapy. It is written for all psychotherapists interested in finding
out about developmental issues. The reader who is not familiar with
the clinical theory of relational psychotherapy will find in the first
chapters a synthesis of its main features. This should allow him to
read and make wise clinical use of the chapters on the main developmental issues.

CHAPTER ONE

Developmental issues in the etiology of personality disorders

The definitions of personality disorders in the DSM help us to form a clinical picture of how enduring and ego-syntonic psychopathology arises. This multi-axial system is the basis of and framework for classification in American empirical psychiatry.

This methodology has some disadvantages. In order to separate personality disorders from clinical syndromes, the American Psychiatric Association (APA) has had to opt for an empirical epistemology designed to allow communication between clinicians of varying disciplines. However, this has meant giving up a whole heritage of knowledge that has been constructed over the last century, that of traditional psychodynamic and developmental epistemology. The DSM may well allow us to diagnose from verifiable observation, but it is of no use when it comes to understanding the etiology and the psychic function of a personality disorder.

These pathologies seem to be sufficiently specific in character for us to be able to distinguish them from Axis I disorders, and place them on Axis II. Let us examine their characteristics: they are generally present from early adulthood, tend to be ego-syntonic, and appear in a variety of contexts. They are woven into the very identity of the person: hence their name of personality disorders. Since these are intimately connected with the identity of the individual, we must understand that the person is immersed in what both defines him and is also the source of his suffering. Nowadays we cannot approach these complex structures of identity in a one-dimensional manner. Personality disorders are the result of several etiological factors, of nature and of nurture, genetic and psychological, as well as risk and resilience factors, present in the person and in his developmental environment.

It seems that as our knowledge of development has increased, each of the areas of study or perspective necessary to our understanding of personality disorders has developed parallel to each of the others. Recently, attempts towards a dialogue have been established between these different perspectives; however, we are still a long way away from a synthesis of theories of socialization, psychodynamics, and applied neuroscience. Nevertheless, it is possible to design a hypothetical model of the system of interactions between factors implicated in the development of personality and in the pathogenesis of personality disorders. This is shown in figure 1.

Let us suppose that the development is a field phenomenon (Lewin, 1951), in the Lewinian sense, that is to say that the individual

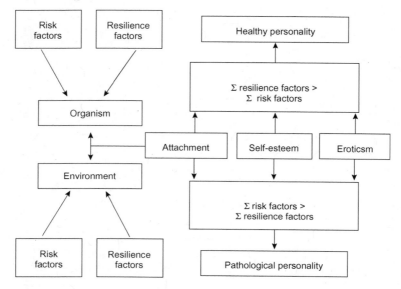

Figure 1. Multi-factorial development.

is subject to the convergence of a multitude of forces that make him who he is. This developmental field is where the psychophysiological organism, the becoming person, meets the environment: human, physical, economic, social, and cultural. The psychophysiological organism is mobilized through an individual's genetic programme and through a human evolutionary blueprint. In chapter Three we will look more closely at early developmental influences and drives. Whatever the original drive of the organism it must develop in a multifaceted and multidimensional environment. One might say that development results from the interaction between the organism and its environment. But, each of the two poles of the organism-environment field carries elements which Lewin might have labelled accelerators or brakes. These either encourage or hold back development. Drawing on the ideas of Boris Cyrulnik (2000), we call the brakes "developmental risk factors" and the forces of acceleration "resilience factors". From this we can make out a matrix of interactions between four groups of forces in the developmental field.

Into the group named "risk factors inherent in the organism", one might add character styles, which are the subjects of contemporary study, and could be linked with the appearance of a personality disorder. Character is defined as being one's style of behaviour. Thus, character does not determine what one does (behaviour) nor why one does it (motivation), but how one does it (Cloninger, Svrakic & Przybeck, 2000). What should we understand by "genetic singularity of character"? By way of example, Cloninger, Svrakic and Przybeck identify four interacting character traits that give each person his personal temperamental style. These are the avoidance of pain, seeking novelty, dependence on reward, and persistence.

Panksepp (1998) names four major systems that organize emotion: the search for pleasure and enjoyment, anger and rage, fear and anxiety, panic and distress. These systems are evolutionary. At the dawn of time, they were necessary for the survival of the individual and of the species. They are "economical" in the sense that they permit an automatic response to biologically significant events. People's individual character styles come from constitutional variations and differences between individuals.

As a result of research on genetic inheritance, we have been able to connect certain character styles with various personality disorders.

Thus we can say that inherited characteristics may constitute both a mixture of risk factors and resilience factors inherent from birth in the psychophysiological organism.

The same is true of the environment which also carries a particular configuration of risk and resilience factors: parental mental and physical health, living conditions, education, social and political upheavals, etc. Therefore, in each chapter on the major developmental issues we will be taking account of these risk and resilience factors.

Thus, development is a result of the meeting between a psychophysiological organism and its environment, each of which carries risk and resilience factors. The growing Self develops by taking in this environment, firstly through parental figures, then by contact with the wider environment, which is less mediated by the parents. Likewise, endowed with an evolutionary blueprint, the little human being has the tools necessary for movement, for grasping and using objects, for walking and talking. If his/her genetic potential carries a greater ratio of resilience to risk factors, s/he will have a greater chance of accomplishing these tasks. The same is true of the environment. The little human being will achieve more if his/her environment carries more resilience than risk factors.

But what needs to be achieved? The task is vast! Firstly, to become a person. At best, to become a person equipped with the ability to live *their* life, having extracted the vital substance from life experiences and having eliminated from these same experiences that which is toxic. There exist many theories as to the diverse resources and skills that will give a person the physical health and robustness necessary for accomplishing their potential. Some people suggest that the basis of mental health is emotional security. Others speak of narcissistic balance, yet others of ego strength. Finally, some follow Freud and put it all down to two fundamental abilities: to love and to work (Erikson, 1968).

I propose that we organize these multiple tasks around three main developmental areas: attachment, self-esteem, and eroticism. This perspective allows us to bring together a broad background of knowledge resulting from infant and early childhood observation, case studies of adult psychotherapy patients as well as empirical and theoretical research.

Over and above any disagreements and semantic differences, this proposed organization of various strands of knowledge about developmental processes allows us to be able to draw upon a clinically useful body of knowledge without engaging in any theoretical conflict. We can now put forward the framework for the rest of our discussion: psychic development is a field phenomenon where a psychophysiological organism meets an environment and this field contains both risk and resilience factors. It takes the shape of a developmental path whereby there are three major developmental tasks that need to be accomplished. Thus we can state that personality disorder is a result of a failure to complete one or several of the developmental tasks and that the signs of this unfinished business can be observed in the phenomenology of a specific pathology. We can establish the following hypothesis: the inability to complete a particular developmental task results from a configuration of the developmental field that can be expressed in the equation:

The sum of the risk factors > the sum of the resilience factors = personality disorder.

In other words, the sum of the risk factors in the developmental field, in both organism and environment, is greater than the sum of the resilience factors.

This would equate with the ongoing observations that most clinicians make. We see people who come from an apparently supportive environment, who in adulthood are obviously suffering from a personality disorder. Conversely, we meet those who have lived in an extremely deficient environment, who are perfectly healthy.

Since the publication of Cyrulnik's work, we have a better understanding of resilience factors which, alongside the more easily recognized risk factors, play a part in each individual's specific developmental trajectory. If the developmental pathway can be seen in this light, and we accept that personality disorder is the result of a preponderance of risk over resilience factors, organic as well as environmental, we are in a better position to understand the ability of the healthy adult to manage the ups and downs of existence without a build-up of serious mental illness.

Getting through infancy with an embryonic form of an adult Self is the result of passing a series of tests, of resolving a series of enigmas or developmental problems which will inevitably occur at various stages as the person matures. We will give the name *developmental issues* to each of the axes of maturation, which begin in early infancy, and which prepare us to face the great existential questions: How shall I survive? What of the Other? Why trust? How shall I love or hate? How and why shall I leave? How and why shall I stay? How can I be free and committed, free and attached? And many other questions!

The psychological function of the developing person can be represented metaphorically as the psyche's immuno-metabolic system. It is therefore the psychic equivalent of the digestive, metabolic, and immune systems. Its job is to take from the environment the psychic nourishment necessary to ensure health and continuing development. One can have "favourite foods", for example, solitude, without becoming schizoid. But no one is perfectly safe and immune from everything. Each personality contains, beyond simple preferences, specific vulnerabilities (uncertainty for the obsessive; isolation for the dependent, and so forth).

The personality develops in a way that requires it to resolve, as best it can, a certain number of developmental issues. Good psychological functioning results from the resolution of each of these issues (Johnson, 1994).

Adulthood is therefore characterized equally by a broad and flexible menu of "favourite foods" or sought-out experiences that have been absorbed, and by a capacity to metabolize life's events in a way that extracts vital energy. This flexibility and maximum resolution of issues does not mean that there will be no sadness, no uncertainty, no tension and confusion in our lives, and neither will we necessarily be nice, affectionate people. It simply means that the personality is sufficiently exempt from structural defects and does not produce serious endogenous clinical problems such as depression, hypochondria, etc.

This said, even well-supported people may suffer situational psychological problems that require professional intervention. This may happen, for instance, if stress factors are so intense that the metabolic and immune systems of the psyche are overwhelmed. Anyone can get food poisoning without having a structural malfunction in the digestive system.

Pathology in the structure of the personality is the consequence of a setback in one or more developmental areas. The pathological personality is characterized not only by a serious deficit in its "digestive, metabolic, and immune" capacities, but equally by the fact that these deficits mirror a person's preferences or "favourite foods": the narcissist wants constant praise yet he metabolizes it as though it were envy and thus confirms an affective isolation where appreciation from another person is never nourishing. In adulthood, one or more incomplete developmental issues seem to persist. The person tries to configure his world so that these issues can be resolved. Yet, instead of resolving them, he keeps finding himself at an impasse. This impasse is paradoxical because it is painful yet it also pre-configures the world according to previous experiences: I am in pain, but at least life is not absurd and senseless, for this experience is familiar.

One recognizes the unconscious need of the paranoid personality to be betrayed, for the narcissist to be envied, for the dependant to be abandoned. In short, a developmental issue lies dormant. These developmental issues are crucial and linked indissolubly to the human condition. When one of them cannot be completed, the experience of rupture or of failure for the young child is totally intolerable. This is why, in adulthood, the person suffering from a structural personality disorder must not let himself know the deep nature of the issue and its incompleteness. The paranoid does not recognize his need to be betrayed, the narcissist does not know why he needs to be envied, and the dependant has no suspicion of his need for abandonment. Rather, each of these experiences is consciously abhorred.

Figure 2 is a diagram of the relationship between the original organism, the early human environment, the developmental issues, and the personality disorder.

On the basis of this diagram, it is very tempting to make unequivocal links between a given issue and a specific pathology: confidence issue = paranoid personality; self-esteem issue = narcissistic personality, etc. We must resist the temptation to do this. Anyone who has worked over time with people presenting with personality problems knows that things are not that simple. Often we find that behind a narcissistic personality, for example, hides an absence

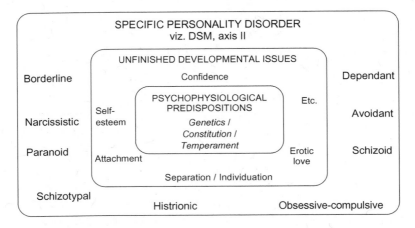

Figure 2. Developmental issues and personality pathology.

of basic security, which a stable and reliable parental figure would have provided. The apparent narcissism compensates for the inability to connect with a reliable Other. The person seeks admiration in order to induce the other to fuse with him. In this way, the desire for the Other is an *ersatz* attachment and a psychic prosthesis—an artificial limb whose role is to fill the void.

Thus, in personality disorders, a developmental issue lies fallow. It is unfinished, in the Gestalt sense of the word. We would be wrong to believe that this old issue has become an archaeological site, suspended in time because work has stopped.

In fact, the person carries this unfinished issue because it is indispensable to him. He is bound to keep finding it in significant areas of his life. Not only does he give personal significance to life events, as cognitive psychology teaches us, but he still goes about actively re-creating conditions that parallel the themes of what is unresolved. Thus he sets up situations where incomplete developmental themes recur. He is confronted anew by the complexity and the pain of attachment, of self-esteem, of separation, of individuation. The person who presents with a personality disorder produces and reproduces, time and again in his life, impasses that are not simply a result of a misreading of reality. These impasses are happening in the here and now. They are real events and experiences, lived within relationships that are equally real.

So, what is the function of these impasses, largely produced and given meaning by the person himself? To understand this, we must understand that a developmental issue lies dormant because it cannot be completed in any conscious way. In fact, a question and a problem still remain, waiting for a response. Instead of consciousness and experiential completion we have dilemma and impasse. In other words, in adulthood, the person keeps returning to the unresolved dilemma and to the subjective distress that accompanied it. Here is the paradox: pain from the past is felt again in the present and deplored, but is cut off from its significant origin, and the person is conscious of nothing apart from having to endure it. Yet at the same time, this pain carries with it a kind of consolation: it gives a sense of being alive. The paranoid may be in considerable distress, surrounded by malevolent people, yet this malevolence makes life predictable, it makes sense of his vigilance and gives it a purpose.

We will not dwell on the so-called masochism of the repetition compulsion (Freud, 1920). A person does not reproduce the impasse and the dilemma just to turn his life into a maze-like prison. He does it hoping, with more or less awareness, that one day someone will show him the way out of the maze. However, for that to happen, he must continually rebuild it. To sum up, repetition has two aims: maintaining a meaning or sense and attempting to complete an experience. From this one can imagine that it is possible to appreciate the severity of a personality disorder on a continuum. The more a person tries to reproduce his impasses (in order to maintain a limited meaning and make completion impossible), the worse the disorder. On the other hand, the more open the person is to new ways of completing the experience, the less severe the disorder.

To present psychological suffering inherent in personality disorders in this way provides the markers for the therapeutic process. We will look at this process in the next chapter.

CHAPTER TWO

Relational psychotherapy

Object Relations Gestalt Therapy (ORGT) evolved from the integration of concepts from British Object Relations into Gestalt-therapy. Those clinicians that have adopted this system wish to use the well-documented capacity of Gestalt-therapy to increase their patients' experiential understanding while maintaining the search for meaning so necessary to the human spirit. This system formalizes dialogic Gestalt practice applicable to personality disorders as defined by DSM.

ORGT believes that psychological health comes not only from creative adjustment in the immediacy of the felt sense (GT) but from a tendency for the Self to embrace its own continuity and to establish in itself an irreversible felt sense of otherness (OR). In order for the individual who suffers from a personality disorder to achieve this state, he/she must disentangle a series of experiential impasses of which that individual understands only the consequences, rarely the process, never the causative issues.

In this chapter the reader is invited to explore the theoretical foundations of this approach, of how its conception of normal development and pathogenesis were arrived at and how they fit the therapeutic model. This is dealt with in detail in *La relation d'objet en Gestalt-thérapie* (Delisle, 1998).

Theoretical basis

Relational psychotherapy is founded on Lewin's field theory, as contained in Perls, Hefferline, and Goodman (1951). Their claim is that psychological facts can only be understood in relation to the wider field. That is to say that ORGT is anything but a "one-minded psychology". Whereas some developmental theories assert that the mother is a universal entity with generic characteristics, ORGT seeks to understand exactly which individual mother we are talking about. The field, as discussed in the previous chapter, is the dynamic interaction between an individual and his material, sociological, economic, philosophical, and metaphysical environment.

Development

The focus of ORGT is to assert that the normal role of the psycho-physiological organism is to develop the Self. This embryonic Self must become a contacting process for metabolizing experience, creating figures, and making meaning. It develops by progressively taking in the field.

At birth, the individual is a unitary psychophysiological organism, with cognitive, affective, and sensori-motor potential that can evolve in a favourable human environment. It is in this environment that early experience finds meaning. This Self is composed essentially of human relationships or internalized object relations.

From the beginning of life, the process of internalization starts with a rudimentary observation of the environment. Later, the language of the human environment, the parents' language, begins to take shape and make sense. Language acquisition is one of the first signs of internalization of the Other. As it develops, the Self progressively internalizes the environment and may do this in two ways: introjection and assimilation. The Self assimilates experience, taking in what is nourishing and eliminating what is harmful or toxic. The assimilated, metabolized elements give it its psychic energy, in the same way as eating supports the physiological organism.

The healthy Self is made up of assimilated internalizations, which remain accessible to the conscious mind. The elements of the internalized field take on the function of adaptable guides in phases of contact and offer psychic protection against elements that are toxic to the Self. Our fundamental security, our self-esteem, and our ability to love come from adaptive learning, experience, and early relationships.

ORGT believes that personality disorder results from unassimilated early developmental experience. In the process of assimilation, a dilemma occurs when the field is organized so that an experience is indispensable, yet intolerable and therefore cannot be assimilated. Thus it is impossible for the young Self to form a clear figure, make sense of it, assimilate and metabolize it. The only answer is to introject the experience. In this way, the person is left with the indispensable without the awareness that it is intolerable. Introjection is a way of internalizing whereby we take in something from the environment without savouring it, chewing it, or spitting out what is indigestible. Take the classic example of eating a peach. You have to bite it, find the stone, chew the flesh, and throw away the stone. In physical terms, introjection would mean swallowing the whole fruit, which would be fairly challenging for an adult. For a child, a developing Self, this would be a seriously unhealthy and physically impossible thing to attempt. The same is true of psychic internalization. An experience introjected in this way allows one to have the indispensable "fruit" (relationship, experience, attachment, etcetera) without realizing that there is an intolerable "stone" (Self-annihilation, humiliation, etcetera). Metaphorically, the introjected object stays in the stomach undigested. Even though it is in us, it is not part of us, as a properly assimilated experience would be. It is a foreign body. An experience that would normally end in assimilation and metabolization is thus interrupted and remains unfinished.

The result is loss of the unified Self. Enduring relational experiences, microcosms of the field, are taken wholesale into the Self. They "live" but are out of awareness. They form an unconscious mass, yet are dynamic and alive.

These microcosms, introjected at the primary stage of life, are called Introjected Microfields (IMs). All enduring relational experiences resulting from a failure of contact are IMs. They are stored and maintained out of awareness in the ground, since awareness would be intolerable. From this ground, out of awareness but still dynamic, they contaminate the process of figure formation and may be mistaken for the external field. In psychotic states, they may substitute for the external field, as the person really believes he is experiencing "out there" a drama that is taking place "inside him".

Early introjection of an experience (made up of the environment, the Self, and the contact between them), simultaneously unassimilable and indispensable for survival, is the blueprint for pathogenic unfinished business in personality development. In order to distinguish these prototypes from other unfinished situations that do not result from this contact dilemma and remain accessible to consciousness, they will be written in italics and in capital letters: *Unfinished Situations (US)*.

These are incomplete relational experiences defined more by their longevity than by moments of contact. Other unfinished situations may mark our development. They may be unpleasant, or painful, but insofar as we can recall them and remember their effects on us, they are tolerable and we do not act them out unconsciously in our here and now experiences.

Development is not just about an early stage in life. It is a continuing life-long process. There are many contributing factors. They exist in the field and come together during crucial contact episodes. Therefore, as we have seen in the previous chapter, development is linked to our genetic inheritance (with its recognized stages of physiological maturation), to our individual hereditary baggage, to our constitution and temperament. It is also linked to the particular contact styles of our parents (reflecting their histories and internalizations), to developmental "accidents", and to the social and cultural environment where the process of socialization takes place.

The functions of the self: id, ego, and the Matrix of Field Representations

Gestaltists are familiar with the concept of the id. Though taken from the psychoanalytic tradition, the id in Gestalt does not carry the same weight or importance as the Freudian id. The id in Gestalt is not a structure of the psyche but a function, a moment in the selfing process. In ORGT, the id retains a part of its function of the dynamic unconscious, in that, as well as being the moment when the Self emerges in the course of a contact cycle, it is the container, in pathological cases, for an unconscious structure in which the IM resides. The id is thus the container for unfinished situations (*US*), or those introjected microfields, which are its basis, and for the energy which these continue to carry.

The ego ensures the relationship between the Self and the environment and is the intermediary between the id and the Matrix of Field Representations (MFR). It has led to the *US* or fixed Gestalt and sometimes, but subordinately, to modify it. The ego therefore eliminates other possibilities in order to maintain the integrity of the Introjected Microfields (IMs) and acts to ensure that those elements of the field that might invalidate an IM remain underneath, while those that might confirm it emerge more easily as a figure. More concretely, the ego reproduces experiences similar to those that have been interrupted, that remain incomplete and kept out of awareness. We will see later what makes these operations necessary. Fig. 3 illustrates the different functions of the Self as it appears in ORGT.

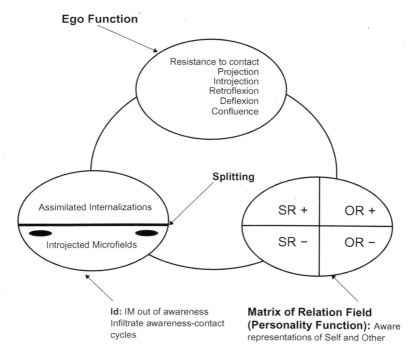

Figure 3. Personality disorders: the damaged self.

The ego regulates the exchanges between the Self and the environment, the internal and external. It essentially uses a regulation system that comprises five modes. In healthy systems these various regulatory modes act as a team: they relay each other and combine together to reach creative adjustment between the Self and the environment, whereas in pathology they result in the repetition of chronic experiential impasses. Confluence involves not differentiating between the internal and external. Projection is the belief that the internal is external. Introjection is thinking the external to be internal. Retroflection is preventing the internal touching the external. Finally, deflection involves preventing the external from touching the internal.

For example, in her contact with certain men Mrs C projects that they are only thinking about "one thing". Thus she introjects every look, every remark, every gesture that might confirm that projection. At the same time she deflects anything from the other that might indicate that things are more complicated than her projection, that there is more to it than just "one thing". And, she retroflects the expression of her own complexity. Absorbed in her own preoccupation, she makes of the relational field a sort of microclimate centred on her theme. The other person feels more or less clearly that who he is or what he does is introjected, while another part is ignored, deflected. In truth, in Mrs C's eyes the other person doesn't exist, except insofar as he is only thinking about "one thing". To a greater or lesser extent Mrs C has got yet one more proof: "men" really do only think about "one thing".

The most crucial of these losses of meaning, seen so clearly in personality disordered clients, is the inability to define where a phenomenon is happening, where an experience is being lived, as well as the inability to link the internal with the external in any meaningful way.

The Matrix of Field Representations (MFR) is marked by the representational residues of contact cycles, including those that have been contaminated by IMs. It is a matrix of potentially conscious representations of the field which reproduces, on the intrapsychic plane, the constituent elements of the field, representations of the Self and of the Other. Each may take on one of the two basic attributes of the general theory of contact: nourishing or toxic. In this way, each person sees the world from the point of view of this matrix: what's good about him/herself; what's bad about him/herself; what's good about the Other; what's bad about the Other. One might imagine that Mrs C interprets the MFR like this:

> "The Other is bad because he only sees women as sexual objects. Very rarely, the Other is good (but it is very rare) because he does not sexualize relations between men and women. I am a woman and I am obliged up to a point to play the game in this macho world."

Impasses in contact and personality disorders

The above example shows that IMs are maintained through relationships in the present field. These IMs, object relations internalized pathologically, entail a lack of spontaneity and creativity in the workings of the Self. The more of these split structures that the Self carries, the more the pressure is generated at an unconscious level on actual experience and the more the Self seeks out the pathogenic experiences that the IMs are demanding.

When the process is an unhealthy one, it is the IMs that animate experience. The drives of IMs must be camouflaged, or there is an intolerable risk of their coming into awareness. When an emerging experience is driven by an IM, there is an incomplete situation operating in its ground to give it energy. This emerging experience is more complex than others and must be seen as distinct and specific, the beginning of a very much more complex process.

Personality disorders may be defined as a constellation of conservative behaviours and attitudes whose function is to preserve the introjected field by seeking out and generating in various experiential fields, contact and relational configurations capable of maintaining dynamic thematic links with unfinished situations from the developmental past. This customary way of functioning is restricted, inflexible, chronic, and is characterized more by conservative than creative adjustment. All the functions of the Self are involved in this.

In those with personality disorders, the sequences of significant contacts begin with the infiltration of an IM into the emerging Id and are maintained by the Ego, through the unconscious use of five modes of contact regulation. They are confirmed by the reinforcement of representations in the MFR.

We must think in terms of etiology about these crucial episodes of contact and about the nature of contact difficulties. In doing so we must consider three parameters. At which stage of psychophysiological maturity does a US (fixed Gestalt) appear? What was the developmental issue? In what way has the person been hindered in his development?

The therapeutic process of ORGT

In the therapeutic relationship the therapist must represent the Other and receive, treat, absorb, and metabolize the impact of the patient[1] or the client. He must start from the hypothesis that the client tends to re-create, in therapy as in other significant relationships, situations that match his unfinished developmental issues. Knowing that clients with personality disorders do this, the therapist must be prepared to "be part of the problem". That the therapeutic relationship in which the client unwittingly re-creates his personal difficulties is the very relationship that is supposed to be helping him makes it a complex business. However, because the therapeutic relationship offers a chance to reactivate unresolved developmental issues, it also contains the potential to repair them.

The therapeutic relationship is an amalgam of three relational modes: the real, the transferential, and the hermeneutic. Each fragment, each episode in therapy may include any of them, in varying proportions. But each of the relational modes is necessary for the completion of another trilogy, the therapeutic trajectory. If it is indeed the case that the client tends to reproduce, unwittingly and in significant relationships, unfinished developmental issues, the job of the therapeutic relationship is to allow these to be completed. I call this restoration. The therapeutic relationship seems to involve cycles of repetition, recognition, restoration.

Thus the best outcome of a therapeutic cycle would be to allow sufficient repetition of a developmental issue (made up of its experiential, representational, and behavioural corollaries). Restoration encourages full recognition of this repetition. However, the cycle is not properly finished until the developmental issue is completed. This is restoration.

Sometimes the possibility of repeating the issue with the hermeneutic effort to find the meaning agreed mutually between client and therapist is enough to bring restoration. Often completion depends on the therapist's response to the client's impasse as it overlaps with repetition. Restoration can only come from the real relationship, the person of the therapist. So, each of the three modes of relating is part of the treatment of the impasse: repetition plays out in the transference, recognition in the hermeneutic, and restoration in the real relationship. The stages of this "trimodality" are like the cycle of contact, observable in a single session as well as in the whole of the therapeutic journey.

I think that any therapist who is trying to help a client with a personality disorder, who sees himself "sitting beside" the client psychologically, entirely concerned with helping him face his problems, is going about it the wrong way. As long as the therapeutic relationship is only concerned with helping, a crucial part of the pathological dynamic is "off screen" and the client cannot express his full complexity. Often he concludes more or less consciously that his experiential complexity is an illusion and if he is going to benefit from therapy he will have to be "simpler". He may also conclude that what he carries within him is so bad that even his therapist cannot cope with it.

Once the intimate experience of the pathological personality is revealed and the resulting therapeutic project is clear, the therapist must show himself to be open to the client's individual complexity. His openness must be based on tolerating the repetition of impasses in the therapy, coping with the client's perceptual distortions about him and with the psychological pressure that this entails. If the therapist clings to his identity and refuses to take the role that the client needs him to take in the repetition of the impasse, then the client's developmental needs and the reactivation of his issues will be hindered. What should have been a therapeutic relationship is reduced to an ongoing problem-solving relationship.

Experiential fields: from here and now to there and then

Clients transfer from one field to another the properties of exchanges or their inner experience of exchanges in a particular field. How does it happen that the client speaks to the therapist like a judge? Or that he expects his partner to listen to him like his therapist does? What is happening in the here and now between client and therapist that causes the memory of a quarrel with his younger brother to be evoked? How can we understand that he felt cruel and unyielding, because as he tells it, it was the other way round?

Every therapist can list the unconscious transfers that clients make during therapy. Gestalt-therapy was originally known for its here and now approach, but Gestalt therapists are no longer prisoners of the present and have recognized the importance of time and space in human experience and in the work of therapy. The therapeutic relationship (here and now), current relationships (there and now), and past relationships (there and then) must all be addressed.

If the here and now deserves special attention, it is because it has the advantage of letting the clinician observe directly how contact cycles are played out, and hence, the dynamic of the three functions of the Self. As he is in the present field, the therapist, directly or indirectly, is affected by contact cycles contaminated by IMs. By combining the two possible values of time and space, we obtain a matrix of four space times. Given that each of these "experiential fields" may be considered as having an internal face and an external face, we can say that there are eight space-time fields in psychotherapy. See table 1.

Personality disordered clients are often unable to discriminate between experiences in different fields. They may have problems addressing some of them or be unable to see links between them. Some clients deny the internal field or the reality of an inner world and want to "stick to facts". Others are so interested in their inner experience that they neglect what is happening in the external field. Others "can't see the connection" between the different fields of their experience and cannot understand how they contribute to creating that which they deplore.

In field theory the past is not denied. But it is not the historic past that is at stake but the past as it acts upon the configuration of the present field. When we are working with a 40-year-old client to dissolve an IM originating in a contact dilemma experienced at age five, we do not try to dissolve something that happened 35 years ago, but something that has been repeating over –35 years.

Optimal psychological functioning is reached when someone is able to distinguish what is happening in his "inner world"

Table 1.   The eight experiential fields.

	External level	Internal level
Here and now	The immediate therapeutic contact that is observable by a reasonable and trustworthy third person.	The internal representations of the therapeutic relationship.
Here and then	An event or sequence in the past history of the therapeutic relationship, observable by a reasonable and trustworthy third person.	The internal representations of the historical moments in the therapeutic relationship.
There and now	The contacts and the significant relationships in the present life of the client, observable by a reasonable and trustworthy third person.	The internal representations of current relationships.
There and then	The contacts and significant relationships in the past history of the client, in particular those of childhood such as might have been observed by a reasonable and trustworthy third person.	The internal representations of past relationships.

(the internal field) from what is occurring in the current field, and when they can recognize links between contact episodes in different space-time fields, internal and external, and recognize and reduce the experiential dissonance between the internal and external when necessary. The experiential psychotherapist must, therefore, be a master of transitions in a therapeutic world that may undergo many permutations. He must guide clients in the experiential exploration of their internalization-externalization processes in the various fields of their existence and, above all, in the therapeutic relationship itself. The therapist's task is to support clients to increase their capacity to be aware of the processes whereby they repeat their IMs and their *US*s in various areas of their lives. To do this, the therapist must develop the ability to see the connections that clients miss, and bring them to their joint attention.

The work of recognition and multimodal integration

No therapist could set off on the adventure of discovering a client's developmental issues equipped solely with clinical flair and a good sense of direction. Great explorers and mapmakers have blazed trails to help us reach this murky world. They are not motorways but they do exist. From the early days of psychology and psychoanalysis, these writers have asked questions, according to their own preoccupations, each nourished or limited by the era in which they lived. The history of theories that seek to understand how we "become who we are" and how it happens that we are "so alike yet unique and irreplaceable", is a real saga. The legacy is so great that one cannot embark upon it without drowning in a sea of contradictions. For example, in order to answer the question "How do we love?" we have to define love. Is it a drive? The result of our need for food being satisfied? A defence against the fear of death? A representation in individual consciousness of the need to reproduce? According to whether one consults Freud, Klein, Fairbairn, Bowlby, or Winnicott, the answers will be different, even contradictory (Silverman, 1986).

This diversity does not detract from the work of those whose theories have stood the test of time. To hope for a definitive answer would be to confuse the epistemology of the natural with the human sciences. Science, art, and philosophy converge in the "quest for meaning" which is actually the "creation of meaning".

This is why ORGT shares the view of most contemporary writers (APA, 1994; Gedo, 1986; Millon & Klerman, 1986) that there is no established etiology for any mental problem apart from organic mental illnesses. Clinicians and theoreticians are divided over several etiological hypotheses, but none has been sufficiently persuasive to become dominant (Millon & Klerman, 1986). It is not surprising that etiological theories have developed concurrently: they deal with human things, with reasons more than causes. They take the position of seeing flaws that need to be corrected and these corrections are often extended to the point that they claim to take into account all psychic phenomena.

Freud took this line himself. Then Melanie Klein, noting that the children that she worked with seemed to give more energy to constructing their interpersonal world than to controlling drives, postulated that the most important development, including the Oedipal dynamic, happened well before the age of four or five years as was suggested by Freud. Then Kohut made narcissism not merely a stage between autoeroticism and object relating, but a separate developmental track. Winnicott, Fairbairn and other classical writers make similar points.

Contemporary psychology is not short of developmental theories. What is needed then is not the construction of yet one more theory but rather the creation of a framework that allows us to make use of the knowledge of psychic development inherited and shaped from early psychoanalysis. ORGT is based on immediate experience, recognizing that this is the container for the individual's history, which is enacted in present experience. ORGT is not bound to any of the usual theories of psychic development and consequently, from this impartial position, ORGT can appreciate a variety of developmental theories for their intrinsic value without becoming bogged down by particular schools of thought or any institutional leanings. It would be hard, for instance, to understand narcissistic vulnerability without Kohut's theory, or to comprehend the constant need to repair an imagined wrong done to another without Klein's contributions.

Faced with the conceptual and clinical challenges of personality disorders, ORGT takes the view that pathology is a mechanism for making sense of a developmental deficit, for masking it, and for activating it in an ambivalent effort to untangle it. ORGT invites the practitioner to give up trying to establish oversimplified links between specific developmental issues and equally specific personality disorders. Instead of offering reassuring and mistaken evidence, clinician and client work at making sense of the client's experience. A dialogic presence puts the therapist alongside the client's impasses, the only place from which they can be disentangled.

Through this informed look at the unique life of the client and by an open- mindedness towards different etiological theories that are varied and complementary, the therapist provides the best conditions for co-constructing the meaning of the experience. With the client, the therapist will revisit unresolved issues and through their unique meeting and the unexpected aspects of the dialogue the client may hope to find his true form.

Note

1. The choice of the term to designate the person who calls on the services of a psychotherapist remains problematic. Since Rogers (1951) the term client is common among humanistic and existential therapists, while the term patient remains common in psychiatry and in certain psychoanalytical schools. In the Comprehensive Text Book of Psychiatry (Sadock & Sadock, 2000) the term patient is used 4217 times, while the word client appears 77 times and mainly in the context of the Rogerian approach or to designate the client in his role of user of medical services. For my part, I use the word client to designate people who consult and who do not have a significant DSM Axis I pathology, and I reserve the term patient for those who have a significant Axis I pathology or a serious Axis II personality disorder. In general, in order not to induce diagnostic presumptions, in the present text I will stay with the use of the word client.

CHAPTER THREE

Object relations development theories: an overview

Psychoanalysis has sometimes been accused of having become a hermetically sealed system, unwilling to be open to the influence of other approaches. However, even though its history is one of violent theoretical and clinical disputes, such as the huge disagreements between Melanie Klein and Anna Freud, contemporary psychoanalysis is nevertheless pluralistic. Its practice has evolved so much that today one might be justified in asking whether classical analysis in its present form may be threatened with extinction. However, regardless of how it is practised, psychoanalytic theory is today part of our universal heritage. We can reasonably selectively employ certain of its more illuminating points without actually having to adopt the whole of its theoretical basis, framework, and techniques.

In this chapter the reader will be given a quick summary of key psychoanalytic theories of development that will be used to inform the analysis of the essential issues of development in the following chapters. In a notable piece of work in 1983, Greenberg and Michell proposed that these diverse theories could be seen through the lens of their respective strengths and weaknesses, and additionally from the angle of their similarities. These authors approach the plurality of psychoanalytic theory using a preliminary epistemological differentiating tool to answer the question: what came first and what has grown out of it? Greenberg and Mitchell classify psychoanalytical theories of development under three major ideological lines: instinct or drive theories, relational theories, and mixed theories. While this system of classification is not unanimously accepted by the psychoanalytic community, for our purpose it will serve to underline one of the seminal points of object relations developmental theory.

A theory is said to be a drive theory if it postulates that the object, the Other, is a derivative of the "instinctual drive". In other words, "drive" theories hold that the search for the Other is driven by need for satisfaction (through this Other) of basic, fundamental "drives" or needs. On the other hand a theory is said to be relational when it is supposed that the "drive" towards the Other exists primarily in order to meet the basic human need to be in relationship. Freudian theory is of course the original prototype for "drive" theories. As for relational theories Fairbairn (1952) began the epistemological rupture that placed the need to be in relationship as the primary activity of the ego. He saw "drive" as functioning in service of the ego, therefore placing it in a secondary position. One could say, along with Apfelbaum (2000), that whereas drive theories describe sexuality, relational theories are concerned with love. This formula is a little simplistic and does not allow for the more subtle and complex aspects of reality but it is a useful way to characterize the theoretical tonalities that we are going to look at.

Starting with the main ideas of several authors, let us now take a look at the various theories of development that are linked to the concept of "object" in the psychoanalytic tradition. This brief summary cannot possibly give credit to the richness of these theoretical systems. Therefore if the reader wants to engage in more depth with the thoughts of these authors, he or she will find a reference section at the back of this book dedicated to these, which would serve as a starting point for further discovery.

The object in Freudian theory

The notion of an "object" first appeared in Freud's thinking in his "Three essays on a theory of sexuality" (1905). According to Buckley (1986), all subsequent theoretical developments in terms of object relations, whether developments or critiques, find their starting point here. In the section devoted to "sexual perversions" Freud presented ideas that would become his "drive theory". Libido was presented as being to sex what hunger is to eating. Drives are psychic representations of a constant, endogenous source of stimulation that is derived from the excitation produced in a particular organ. Their immediate aim is the satisfaction of these organic stimuli. However, sexual drives must combat the mental forces that act as resistances: shame and disgust. These innate affects emerge to repress or to substitute for several processes and desires. They are emotionally charged and through a psychic process (repression) are unable to emerge into consciousness. As to the object, it is whatever is the target of the drive, whether it be a person, a part of a person, an inanimate object, or an idea. As Freud wrote in "Drive and the destiny of the drive", the object is "that in which or through which the drive can reach its target …. It is not necessarily external and can just as well be a part of one's own body (Freud, 1915, p. 19).

Freud already noticed that sexual drives are perhaps not simply urges but rather are integrated mechanisms that disintegrate or separate in the perversions. If this is the case, the study of perversions should allow one to understand the phenomena that one cannot observe in normal people because of the hidden or unconscious nature of their sexual practices. Later in 1921, in "Group psychology and the analysis of the ego" Freud wrote: "In the individual's mental life someone else is invariably involved as a model, as an object, as a helper, as an opponent" (pp. 1–2).

If we accept this summary of Freud's "sexual drive theory" for the moment, one can conclude that the client clings on to infantile desires and resists recognizing them for what they are. The object of the analysis therefore becomes the resistance to admitting to an unconscious motivation, which, once it is cleared, should permit the client's "ego" to make conscious choices where previously there was only unconscious motivation. In the therapeutic process, the conscious subjectivity of the client counts for little, as the validation of the analyst's interpretations comes from the client's subsequent associations and not from the fact that he consciously accepts these interpretations. This point of view that the post-Freudians find too biologically mechanical (organic excitation, need to discharge, etc.) will nonetheless be useful in order to have a better sense of just what is at stake, developmentally, in the ability to love, in the erotic sense of the word.

Freud himself recognized that he did not become interested in the link between the baby and mother until the end of his work, mainly from his 1931 writing on female sexuality. He admitted to having found it difficult to grasp the importance of the attachment to mother, mainly because his patients developed a "paternal" transference towards him. Freud showed proof of the courage and the epistemological "distance" necessary in order to make this observation, given that at the time all his earlier declarations were considered to be dogma! In his original theory, an infant's anxiety arose from the feelings of threat aroused in him that his primary needs would not be met if his mother disappeared. The heart of the process was therefore not the mother herself or her maternal love but the satisfaction of the primary physiological needs of the infant.

In the tradition of Freudian drive theory, attachment to the mother is firstly driven by the desire for the satisfaction of needs and not desire for a specific object itself. In fact the relationship to the mother is not seen as the first relationship with the environment. This is preceded by an earlier phase during which the world of partial objects develops and where the satisfaction of physical needs plays a decisive role. In this tradition, there is a developmental phase whereby the essential part of psychic life is lived in relationship to the erogenous zones, those through which the drives are expressed and discharged. The object is a far away reality of which one becomes progressively conscious and this consciousness culminates in the resolution of the Oedipal situation.

For Freud, that which gives rise to relationship with the object is the satisfaction of primary needs. When it seems that there is an anxiety due to object loss, it is in fact an anxiety linked to a loss of gratification.

The relational theories

Whereas the "drive" perspective is more concerned with infantile sexuality and need satisfaction, the relational perspective is more of a love story. And the love that we are concerned with here is above all parental—usually mother's—love. Therefore most object relations theories apply above all to understanding the processes by which the relationship is established with the first object of love, the parental figure.

Parental love and the relationship to this first love object takes us away from the organic excitations of the drive theory and gives priority to other realities such as mother's care, becoming attached, discovering the world, and the development of self-esteem. In the general framework of relational theories, these considerations are legitimate and cannot be understood uniquely as derivatives of the "drives". The analyst occupies a different position, as he is theoretically justified in taking on the repressed desires of his patients and not dismissing them as just incestuous transference.

Effectively, as these repressed desires are not made up of libidinal drives towards the parental figures, they do not result in inherent shame or disgust. The need to love, to be loved, to be esteemed, and to feel secure has nothing fundamentally reprehensible and will not, in the framework of relational perspectives, be interpreted as the transformation of an incestuous desire. Where Freud's drive perspective would aim to result in a mature repression and delayed gratification, the relational point of view has no interest in such a delay, in such a holding back. This "holding back gratification" makes no sense in the context of attachment and self-esteem.

In the therapeutic process of the relational perspective it is not a matter of uncovering hidden attempts for gratification, but rather to make possible the gratification of needs for love and self-esteem. The analyst who works within the relational perspective acts in this sense as a "parent" offering a second developmental chance.

Over and above these first distinctions between the drive and relational theories, Apfelbaum (2000) and others believe that one can further categorize the relational theories into "hard" and "soft" theories. Among those that adhere to the "hard" theorists such as Klein, Fairbairn, and Kernberg, there are as many interpretations as among Freudians, but these are still more concerned with the repressed desire for relationships than the defences against these desires.

In the "soft" theories such as those of Winnicott or Kohut, interpretation is less important than the welcome and "holding" (Winnicott) or empathy (Kohut). Basically the patient does not "resist" but seeks, however clumsily, to regain his developmental path. However useful Apfelbaum's typological logic may be, it remains difficult to classify some important theorists such as Mahler, Guntrip and Jacobson.

Let us take a look at some of the authors who can light the way for us, not in order to arrive at a full theoretical analysis or complex clinical application but rather in order to get a general feeling for object relations theories and see what they can bring to our theoretical and clinical integration of theories of developmental pathologies. After Freud, Klein, Winnicott, Fairbairn, and Mahler, other authors will appear but their main ideas will be evoked in relation to specific developmental issues. Those that we will speak of here have a general approach in common which makes them a good place to start for all who wish to deepen this way of considering the development of object relations.

Melanie Klein

The difference between Freudian theory, constructed around the analysis of adult memories, and the Kleinian system is that the latter is the result of clinical work with young children. Melanie Klein noticed very early on that children were not able to work within the adult analytical framework. Their conceptual and verbal capacities are far too limited and above all, they have little ability to relate the present to the past. She used play as the primary therapeutic tool. She discovered that children devote more of their energy to the construction of their interpersonal world than to the control of their libidinal drives. Their internal world is made of internal representations of significant people in their lives. The internal world is, in fact, a world of relationships between internal objects. Here the mother-child relationship constitutes the prototype for all subsequent relationships. However—and it is still a controversial concept in Kleinian theory—the mother exists for the child before birth. She is firstly an endogenous, inborn presence from the womb that guides the child in its subsequent interactions with a real mother.

This is a provocative and interesting idea. Firstly it is based on the fusional reality of pregnancy. The child appears inside the mother, is nourished by her *in utero*, living with her moods, etc. In addition, this idea suggests that the mother was never a stranger for the child to discover and internalize. In terms of field theory, one could say that before being a part of the environment, she was part of the organism! That might help us explain the sometimes rocky nature of the relationships that some clients have with their mothers.

In Kleinian theory, development is achieved through an evolutionary process, starting from the paranoid-schizoid position and ending with the achievement of the depressive position. The first stage takes place in the first six months of life and is characterized by a mental universe that is split between good and bad or between the life instinct and the death instinct. Klein retained the idea of the death instinct even after Freud had abandoned it. For Klein, a powerful internal conflict (between life and death) is present from the beginning of life. It generates an intolerable anxiety and must be projected onto the exterior world. It is this fundamental endogenous conflict that is at the source of the splitting of good and bad in the child. The death instinct is thus projected onto the environment, which, consequently, fills up with "bad objects". In order not to fill up the exterior solely with bad objects the child also projects a part of its libidinal energy into the environment so as to create good objects. All these objects, good and bad, are then re-introjected in order to create an internal representation of the environment, separated into good and bad objects. This dynamic exchange is the basis of the Kleinian perspective of the infantile psyche.

In an effort to live with the death instinct, and the consequent desire to destroy the good, the child must constantly project and introject feelings of hate. The basic psychic conflict is between the feelings of protection and destruction, between the desire to protect mother and the desire to destroy her.

A certain number of relational positions are derived from this conflict and these can be located on a continuum ranging from hate to love. These positions designate a developmental profile from birth to death.

The paranoid-schizoid position

This is the "first position". It covers the first four months of life and is marked by the pain and anxiety associated with birth as well as the loss of the security of the womb. Through this experience of pain and loss, the child feels attacked and persecuted. It is also a time of meeting with the first object; or rather part object, the maternal breast, as well as the first experience of destructive impulses.

It is here that Klein (1978), using the language of *phantasy* that is specific to her, and that even today makes both her followers and her adversaries uncomfortable, speaks of "infantile vampirism" and writes that "the child wants to destroy the breast and is afraid of being destroyed by it".

"Persecution anxiety" is the result of the child's efforts to externalize his anxiety and is the source of considerable torment with which he reacts by separating the good and bad images of the maternal breast: the one nourishing, carrier of good milk and of life, the other vengeful and capable of destroying the infant.

The depressive position

The process of achieving the depressive position is, ideally, a period of rapid psychological growth, between the ages of four and 24 months. The main developmental task of this period is to undo the split and re-establish the mother as a complete and complex object, made up of both good and bad parts.

Gradually, the child understands that good and bad can come from the same person. The mother can then be seen as imperfect, simultaneously good and bad. As the split starts to dissolve, the child must recognize its own negative feelings, including hatred towards the mother. There is, however, a cost in this process. The child, realizing that his hatred was directed towards a whole mother, believes that he has hurt her. There emerge very powerful feelings of guilt that pre-configure the appearance of depressive anxiety. The subjective experience of bad inflicted on the mother and the resulting guilt will later on be transformed into empathy. This guilt and the desire to repair that accompany it signify that a more mature stage of the object relations has been reached.

As we can see, Klein conceived the affective life of the infant as being constructed of very complex mental operations. The Kleinian universe is rich in fantasies, which, in contrast to their role in Freudian theory, are not the result of action but rather invariably precede all human experience.

Today, after more than 60 years, the Kleinian heritage remains solid. Despite the fact that one can deplore that she chose to use a vocabulary borrowed from psychiatry in order to describe a universal mental process centred on the maturation of relational capacities, it remains true that her determination to understand the infantile psyche without colouring it with romanticism, enables us to better understand the tormented internal world of certain patients. Those who work with patients with borderline personalities or pre-psychotic organization are thankful for these explorations of the darker side of the first relational experiences.

Donald Woods Winnicott

Trained as a paediatrician, Winnicott was an English psychoanalyst of the same generation as Melanie Klein, by whom, incidentally, he was supervised towards the end of the 1930s. He also undertook a ten year personal analysis with James Strachey, and after that an additional three or four years with Joan Riviere. For this doctor, interested in the mother/baby dyad, mental health was primarily a reduction of the potential towards psychosis. In his view this psychological solidity depends essentially on the "good enough" mothering.

For Winnicott, the mother is biologically and psychologically prepared, even before giving birth, with a sort of egocentricity or preoccupation. The baby is born into a matrix that we speak of as the mother-baby dyad. A normal devoted mother knows how to hold the infant, how to handle him correctly, and how to introduce the world to him. In return the infant lets her know how he is feeling through his crying or laughter.

In contrast to Klein, Winnicott was not a system builder, but was rather a practical clinician, whose interest was essentially focused on clinical work. His central contribution, which one can consider to be of considerable importance for the modernisation of psychoanalysis, was to identify how the Self develops from a relational matrix. Up to this time, with the Freudian system and what was to become the Kleinian system, psychoanalysis could be described as a "one mind psychology", an individual psychology, almost solipsistic. Winnicott, although he did not use these terms, introduced both the concept of the field and the concept of polarity into the theoretical apparatus of psychoanalysis.

One of the great difficulties with which Winnicott's theory confronts us comes from the fact that most of his written work is derived from oral presentations. This has the disadvantage of not clearly documenting the evolution of his thinking as it related to the psychoanalytical systems of his time. Through this he formulated a rather virulent set of criticisms of Fairbairn, notably reproaching him for having disowned the very foundations of Freudian meta-psychology. In any case, the opinion of many contemporary authors, notably Greenberg and Mitchell (1983) is that Winnicott's loyalty towards Freudian metapsychology is somewhat paradoxical. While professing an unconditional adhesion to Freudian concepts, he redefines them to a point that they are hardly recognizable! In fact, despite his self-acclaimed allegiance towards Freudian and Kleinian metapsychology, the developmental model that Winnicott left us is decidedly more at home in the relational perspectives camp than in that of the drive perspective.

Read from a contemporary perspective, Winnicott's contributions seem to gravitate around the crucial issues involved with relationship as well as differentiation, both being in some respects seen as polarities that define the two ends of a continuum. From a Winnicottian point of view, extreme differentiation is obtained at the cost of relationship with the other. These are the principal fault lines in the cohesion of the Self, those which imperil survival itself.

During his development, the infant first uses the mother's representation of himself as a support. It is through her gaze—partly prism, partly mirror—that the young infant can internalize his first representations of himself and the surrounding universe.

While the infant attempts to organize his perceptions and his representations, proceeding by trial and error through the phases of his physiological maturation, the mother acts as a container for the disorganized fragments and takes care to give them back to the infant in an assimilable form. The mother is thereby the first environment and this environment is seen by Winnicott as "holding environment". To allow for this task, this maternal mission to be successfully accomplished, the mother must be animated by a sort of devotion that exceeds, in intensity and in exclusivity, that which a human being ordinarily can expect of another. In order to describe this specific form of devotion, Winnicott used the term "primary maternal preoccupation". This is the foundation of what he called the "good enough mother".

In addition to containing her infant and his fragmented perceptions, the "good enough mother" presents the world to her baby.

This function of "presenting" also plays a vital role in the infant's development. The mother-baby adjustment is sufficiently good when the infant becomes excited by an emerging need and the mother presents him with an object that is sufficiently adjusted to this need (offering the breast or the bottle, changing a nappy, etc.). The more the mother correctly perceives the emerging need and responds adequately to it, the more the infant's experience of "me-the world" is organized into a coherent whole.

Later, and according to the physiological maturity of the baby, the mother emerges progressively from this exceptional state of devotion and becomes available once again for other aspects of her life. During this journey, which goes from very close proximity to a more separate nature, the members of the mother- baby couple are transformed. During this subtle process, the mother passes through a phase in which her role is to be a presence that does not demand contact with the child if he does not need it. This carefully adjusted and progressive distancing, specifically because it *is* adjusted and progressive, allows the child to build its developmental experience of the capacity to be alone by at first being "alone in the presence of another".

From this space, the child discovers the limits to its power and integrates this reality: the world exists and evolves out of my control! Gradually the child acquires more autonomy and a greater capacity for differentiation, which renders the pain of this realization more bearable. In the best cases, the diminution in the mother's devotion corresponds in intensity to the growing natural need of the child for differentiation and autonomy. During this phase whereby the dynamic of the baby- mother dyad redefines itself, the inevitable difficulties of the mother to adapt to the change are seen as essential to the normal accomplishment of the differentiation. One can say that there is a powerful motivating force contained in the child's disappointment in his mother.

Pathological development, according to Winnicott, finds its origins when a mother has great difficulty adapting herself to the child's needs. Either she is incapable of providing an initial environment that is well enough able to protect the child and to provide the containment necessary for the child's security, or she is unable to correctly regulate her withdrawal from the mother-child matrix. In other words, if she is too close and, by over-anticipating, responds too quickly to the energetic mobilization linked to the need, she prevents the infant from achieving a full representation of his needs and creativity. Or, inversely, if she withdraws too quickly or insensitively she does not allow the developmental discoveries linked to the experience of a comfortable solitude.

It would not be possible, even in a brief outline such as this, not to mention the Winnicottian concepts of "True Self" and "False Self". Winnicott drew a parallel between what Freud called pregenital and genital sexuality and his hypothesis of a central part governed by the "impulses" that he called the True Self and another part that is turned towards the exterior, establishing a relationship with the world: the equivalent of the False Self. He also introduced the idea of false personalities built on a False Self which are precursors of the personality disorders of the DSM.

This said, it is important that we are careful not to believe, despite humanistic conventions, that the True Self is any better than the false! In fact, according to Winnicott, it is more the nature of the relationship between the two that defines health and pathology. This is how Winnicott organizes the False Self: on a continuum from "pathology" to "health", the False Self is felt and presented as real and it is this that observers tend to take for the whole person. However, in stressful situations the person operating from an extreme False Self is often perceived as missing something essential. In this extreme position, there is no access to the True Self. To a lesser degree, the function of the False Self is to protect the authentic Self. The True Self is thereby dissociated and given a secret, hidden life. The advantage of this less than optimal configuration is the preservation of the individual despite the abnormal conditions present in the environment.

In healthier individuals the False Self has the principal objective of seeking, or even creating, conditions that can make it possible for the True Self to exist outside its secret world. An even healthier position is for the False Self to develop on the basis of identification with healthy people. Inspired by this positive identification, the False Self acts as a partial screen, thereby protecting the True Self. Finally, in optimal health, the False Self is represented by all that constitutes a socially acceptable attitude—good manners, a certain reserve, social intelligence, community spirit—that is necessary for harmonious relational functioning. Here a more sophisticated and facilitative False Self has given up a longing for omnipotence and other aspects of "primary process" experience in exchange for a place in society, a place that the True Self would never be capable to reach or maintain without help.

Let us conclude this glance at Winnicott's theory with a summary of the concepts of transitional phenomena and transitional space. Transitional space reveals itself to be in the space between the child's internal and external reality. This is neither an illusion nor reality, but a meeting point between these two worlds. Transitional space allows the child to build a relationship between these two worlds. From this relationship is born the unique nature of the "ego" of the child. As for a transitional object, it enables the child to diminish the gap between the "inside" and the "outside". This object (a blanket, teddy bear, etc.) encourages the emergence of this "space between" from where all creativity, all invention comes forth. The object is the precursor of symbolization, the capacity to grasp the concept of similarity and difference and of the capacity to be alone and to create.

Margaret Mahler

Margaret Mahler was a paediatrician. Before immigrating to the United States she lived and worked in Vienna where she was in analysis with Helen Deutsch. She created a treatment centre for children and she had the opportunity to work with Anna Freud. Mahler was particularly interested in infantile psychosis, being primarily concerned with understanding questions of separation and individuation. She distinguished two fundamental types of infantile psychosis, autism and symbiosis, which she claimed were also aspects of a normal process of infantile development.

In 1975 Margaret Mahler published *Separation and Individuation: The Psychological Birth of the Human Infant*. This work was the fruit of systematic research and observation that respected the empirical research norms of the time. These observations led her to formulate a developmental model whereby the psychic maturation of the human infant is seen as a function of the evolution of relational distance between the child and its mother. For Mahler, "growing away" is a primary attempt to achieve one's individual identity. This process of separation/individuation can last a lifetime. The heart of the process is the journey from a symbiotic attachment to the achievement of an identity that is stable and autonomous.

From birth, according to Mahler, the infant lives in what she called an autistic phase, normally lasting for the first two months of life. The infant exists in a state between sleeping and waking, concentrating more on the physiological realities of life outside the womb than on the relationship with mother or the primary caretaker. On a psychic level, the infant lives as if in a closed system with no awareness of other human beings. The symbiotic stage appears next and lasts until the fifth month. During this period of growth, the mother is vaguely associated with the experience of warmth and satisfaction. The infant starts to smile in her presence, but she is still experienced as a part of the infant's system. During this phase, even if the infant is physiologically satisfied, he may react with distress if the mother is emotionally disturbed.

The developmental phase that Mahler was most interested in was that of separation/individuation. It lasts from the sixth to the 36th month and corresponds to what she called a psychological birth. It is during this phase that the most important existential conflict is played out: the quest for autonomy and the need to stay fused with the mother. The capacity of the infant to eventually function as an adult, to connect with others while remaining differentiated depends on the successful resolution of this conflict. This crucial phase occurs in four sub-phases.

The differentiation phase

The differentiation process begins around the fifth month. With the supporting help of increasing neuro-physiological maturation, perceptual discrimination begins to be more precise. Sight and distance-based contact functions develop and the mother starts to be recognized as a separate entity. If the infant is left in the presence of a stranger, one can observe some signs of anxiety.

The practising phase

At around ten months, the infant starts to crawl. He can therefore choose to move away from his mother. It is during this phase of trying to move away from the mother that Mahler sees the psychological birth of the child. However, the mother remains the "base camp" of the young explorer and the infant regularly checks to see if she is still there.

The rapprochement phase

The phase between the 15th and the 30th month is marked by the rapid development of language, due to a "return" to mother after a period of exploring the world. The child interacts verbally with mother and others, in particular father. It is a phase of separation and of self-affirmation. Overjoyed by his new independence, the little one is almost arrogant in his all-powerful stance, but he still feels an intense need for help and reassurance. The infant's freedom to discover new competencies nourishes his feelings of self-sufficiency, alternating with periods of dependence. This phase is crucial and the optimal response of the mother consists in supplying a balance between emotional support and firmness. A denial of his need for both independence and dependence can derail the "rapprochement" crisis. This can take the form of a struggle between mother's needs and those of her baby.

The object constancy phase

It is around the third year that a stable internal representation of the mother must crystallize. If the child cannot build up this representation then he continues to be dependent on the physical presence of the mother for security and does not develop an autonomous Self. On the other hand, if this phase is successful, the child maintains an internal representation of the mother, even in her absence, which constitutes the foundations of the capacity to establish healthy object relations. This introjection of both negative and positive aspects of the mother have been integrated as a whole, without which the child (and later the adult) will react to the interpersonal world as if it is either punishing, rejecting or gratifying, without a sufficient phenomenological basis that allows for containment of these affective reactions.

W. R. D. Fairbairn

William Ronald Dodds Fairbairn was born in Edinburgh and lived there almost all his life. During the First World War he participated in military action, an experience that had a decisive effect on his life, as one can see from his work on wartime neurosis. He finished his studies in medicine in 1929 and then turned to psychiatry. Geographical distance enabled him to be away from both the bombing of London during the Blitz and the public disagreements that existed at the same time between Anna Freud and Melanie Klein and to write and teach in Edinburgh in relative peace. Little disposed to academic debate, he formulated some fundamental criticisms of Freud's work which could have got him into a few scrapes had he not been cut off from current debates.

While he continued to use the Freudian term "libido", Fairbairn did not believe that it was pleasure-seeking but saw it rather as person-seeking, as searching for relationship. He saw the goal of the libidinal impulse not to discharge, but to establish satisfactory human relationships. In this object-seeking, the child is turned towards reality from the very beginning of his life.

Fairbairn challenged the Freudian idea according to which the newborn infant was driven by impulsive forces, anchored in the erogenous zones. These zones for him were just the channels leading to object relating. In addition, for Fairbairn, when the pleasure resulting from the drive impulse becomes the primary motive, it means that the essential elements of the relationship with another are broken or deteriorated: in these cases the "subject" experiences having failed. He cannot establish and maintain rich and mutual relationships with others, within which the individuality of the other supplies a deeper satisfaction than simply using the other for his own satisfaction.

Fairbairn recognizes in the work of Klein the developmental role of the object, and in a similar way he takes into account the discoveries and the formulations of Freud concerning the super-ego. We are in debt to Fairbairn for his theory of the development of the ego conceived in terms of object relations. This relation to the object is born while the Self of the infant is embryonic and it takes him some time to learn how to make contact and to organize his relationship with the mother.

Fairbairn did not agree with Freud's libidinal developmental phases (oral, anal, and phallic), but rather proposed an object relations developmental model based on variations in dependence on mother. He believed that all children progress along a continuum ranging from infantile dependence to a more mature dependence. This ultimate stage of psychic development is characterized by an interpersonal life, which reflects intra-psychic life, made up of reciprocity and exchanges, illuminated by the recognition of difference and by the acceptance of a healthy dependence. The ego develops therefore at the same time as the state of infantile dependence, based on a primary identification with the object, giving way to a mature dependence, founded on the ability to differentiate between Self and the object.

This process of the ego development is achieved in three phases: that of infantile dependence, which more or less corresponds to the oral phase, the transitional phase, and finally the phase of mature dependence that corresponds to the genital phase. During the infantile phase, the infant lives in a state of psychological fusion with the parent. He is little differentiated and has a little developed embryonic sensation of Self. He must internalize or, in Fairbairn's terms, "interiorise" external objects, undivided in their essence, complete in themselves, reuniting good and bad, satisfying and unsatisfying properties.

The bad aspects of the external objects are internalized through an introjective mode. This is an unusual idea. Why would a child introject the bad object? Why take inside that which is bad? Let us see what Fairbairn says:

> It is important to ask oneself, how bad objects hold their power over the individual. If the child's objects are bad, how does he interiorise them? Why not just simply reject them as he would with castor oil? In fact, generally, the child finds it very difficult to reject castor oil, as some of us may know from personal experience. The child would reject it if he could but we do not give him the opportunity. The same reasons apply to his bad objects. No matter how much he would like to reject them, he cannot escape from them. They impose themselves on him and he cannot resist them because they hold a power over him. He is therefore obliged to interiorise them in an effort to control them. But by trying to control them in this manner, he interiorises objects that had power over him in the external world and these objects conserve their prestige and their power over him in the interior world. In one word, he is possessed by them, as if by bad spirits. And that is not all. The child interiorises his bad objects, not only because they impose themselves on him and he seeks to control them, but also, and above all, because he needs to. If the parents of a child are bad objects, he cannot reject them, even if they do not impose themselves on him,

> because he cannot live without them. Even if they neglect him,
> he cannot reject them, because if they neglect him, his need for
> them is further reinforced (1952, p. 67).

In contrast to Klein, according to Fairbairn, aggression serves the libido, and the child only becomes aggressive because he is frustrated. As in the case of the castor oil, the infant would reject the bad object if he could, but we do not give him the possibility. The bad objects, therefore, impose themselves on him because of their superior power or because they are, despite all, indispensable to survival. Even if the parents reject him, the child cannot escape the fact that he still needs them. In fact, his need for them is increased. He can only internalize them in the hope of controlling them, but their status and their power remain intact in his mind and it is almost as though the child feels possessed by an evil spirit (1954, p. 66).

Once the bad object has been internalized the bad is within and the environment becomes safe again. The bad objects that have become internalized are then repressed. Fairbairn distinguishes two types. The "conditional" bad object, because it is "bad" from a moral point of view, and the "unconditional" bad object because it is bad from a libidinal point of view. These objects are internalized as persecutors and, in as much as the child identifies with them, he feels bad himself. In order to rectify this situation where he is unconditionally bad, the child internalizes his good objects which become the super-ego. And so there is an intra-psychic wrestling match where the good and the bad confront each other from a moral point of view. When the good wins, the child feels conditionally good. When the bad wins, the child feels conditionally bad, but this is preferable to being unconditionally bad, because, as Fairbairn suggests (p. 71), it is better to be a sinner in a world full of saints than a saint in a world ruled by the devil. At least, if the world in which we live is made of goodness, there is hope.

If the repression fails, the ego may develop one or another of four classic defences: the obsessional defence, the hysterical defence, the phobic defence, and the paranoid defence.

The Self, healthy or pathological, can then be seen as emanating from a process of involving many parts of the ego and its object relations.

The process that impedes development, pathologically, involves the efforts of the ego to perpetuate connections and hopes with internal objects. In other words, the pathology is the compensating attachment to internal objects. The internalized and split objects can considerably hinder development. In brief, the essential nature of maturity is the capacity to establish rich, intimate and mutual relationships with the Other. Psychopathology manifests itself through interruptions in the natural sequences of relationship and by a proliferation of relationships with compensatory internal objects rather than with real ones.

How are these compensatory internal objects organized? The psychic structure results from splitting, a universal and pathological phenomenon, which all human beings employ in order to survive the inevitable turbulence of early development. This splitting serves to divide and organize the Self. The Self, when divided, can take in both agreeable and disagreeable aspects of the object keeping them in circumscribed parts of the Self that are attached to the split parts of the ego. This is how the inner world is born. Both the partial and complete objects can then be repressed or projected on to external objects, thereby modulating the exchange between the internal world and the external world, regulating the experience of the one in response to the fluctuations of the other.

Where do the partial objects contained in the Self come from? The mother (or rather the mother's breast) is, originally, a type of "undivided" object that Fairbairn also called the original object. This object, which then becomes divided into two parts under the effects of the love and hatred experienced by the child, will be introjected into the emerging Self. These he called the exciting object constructed through interactions with the mother who teases and tempts the child. When the child (and later the adult) is in relation with the frustrating or rejecting object, frustration and emptiness are the dominant experience. The rejecting object is created by the child through his interactions with the hostile or removed parts of the mother. The figural experience of the child, and then the adult in relation to this internalized, rejecting object, is to feel unloved or undesired. The affect that accompanies this is anger. Fairbairn also believed that there remains a desexualized centre to the Self, the ideal object or the ego ideal, that contains the comforting and gratifying aspects of the breast.

As it is the libidinal, endogenous energy of the ego that enables the discovery of the object and the creation of a connection to it, the ego must be libidinally attached to the object. Due to this attachment, when the object is split, the Self is split too. The preconscious or unconscious interior world thereby ends up finding stability in a system whereby split egos are twinned to their split and partial objects. From the original ego there remains, therefore, a three part structure created of subsidiary egos twinned to split objects, as can be seen in Figure 4, reproduced from Bouchard and Derome (1987).

The central ego, residue of the original ego, is the agent of repression and is responsible for the relationship with the world of real objects. Fairbairn calls it the "I". Despite the fact that Fairbairn particularly underlines its conscious elements, it also contains preconscious and unconscious parts. The libidinal ego is the split and

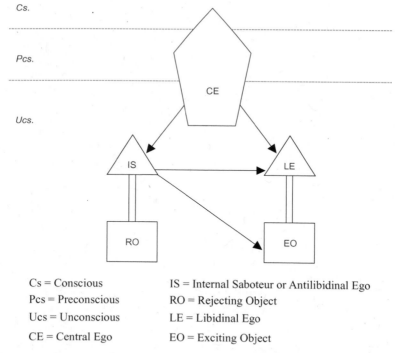

Cs = Conscious	IS = Internal Saboteur or Antilibidinal Ego
Pcs = Preconscious	RO = Rejecting Object
Ucs = Unconscious	LE = Libidinal Ego
CE = Central Ego	EO = Exciting Object

Figure 4. A revised schema of the psyche, adapted from Fairbairn (1944 and 1954).

repressed part of the original ego, the consequence of a split in the object, and it is in a libidinal relationship with the exciting object. It is because of the existence of this libidinal ego and the absence of a death instinct that Fairbairn's model does not need the classical concept of the id, the origin of the drives. We must therefore understand that in Fairbairn's system the libidinal ego serves an analogous function to that of the Freudian id. Finally, the anti-libidinal ego is presented as the split and repressed part of the original ego, in relation with the rejecting object. It is identified with the attacking parents and represents a primary persecutory structure who, later, fuses with the inhibiting aspects of that which Freud called the "ego ideal" and the "super-ego".

For Fairbairn, normal human relationships are fundamentally interpersonal. In this sense he differentiates "interpersonal relationships" and "object relationships". A non-pathological relationship with a real person does not need to be internalized into the Self because the interpersonal interaction is in itself satisfying. Effectively, the emphasis being put on the personal and the interpersonal, it is the failure of the interpersonal which leads to object relations or the establishment of the endopsychic structure. Therefore, for Fairbairn, all these identifications are defensive or pathological and the schizoid state represents the tragic destiny of man, in as much as splitting is inevitable (Grotstein & Rinsley, 1994, pp. 8–11).

For Fairbairn, the Self that manages behaviour in an optimal and adapted manner maintains its integrity against the pressure of subsidiary Selves. These two sets of forces vary according to the history of the person and the nature of the external environment towards which the behaviour is directed (Sutherland, 1994, p. 26).

Finally, Fairbairn believed that the impulse and zonal point of view is so impersonal and inadequate that it might itself well be the product of a schizoid thought process and a result of the personal realities of human life! In other words, Fairbairn, precursor of Kohut, clearly puts the emphasis on external realities.

To sum up …

The psychoanalytic theorists who followed Freud and whose developmental theories we have just explored, all have specific "givens" in common. For one, they establish that the crucial and determining elements of human development occur very early on, perhaps even at the very beginning of life. Next, they accept that this is more to do with the affect of love—and for Klein, hate—than with the discharge of sexual impulses. Finally they attribute to the maternal figure a primordial role in the various phases of early development.

The authors that we have just met are those who have laid the foundation of contemporary schools of psychoanalysis and their heritage remains very much alive in those who have followed them. In this way, Kohut owes much to Winnicott and to Fairbairn and, similarly, Jacobson and Kernberg owe much to Mahler. As for Klein, her theoretical and clinical contributions are even now still being expanded. Her ideas have been taken up, notably by Bion, but also by a large number of contemporary analysts who have developed, particularly, thinking around the concept of projective identification. This area has also been explored by Kernberg (1975, 1998), Ogden (1979, 1982), Langs (1978), and several others.

In what way and how do these theories extend or transform the Freudian canon? We are still trying to answer this thorny question. For our part, let us consider this heritage of knowledge from a point of view of complementarity. These theoretical contributions will be particularly useful when examining what is at stake in the areas of attachment, self-esteem, and erotic love.

CHAPTER FOUR

Attachment issues

The most important developmental issue involved in attachment is the establishment of the basis of our affective security, which forms the basis of the quality and the solidity of our engagement with others. When the attachment process is correctly negotiated, the capacity and the desire for contact and intimacy are installed in the infant. Interdependence then seems natural and it is accepted calmly. Those who have successfully mastered this developmental phase are better able to experience the reality of separations, without developing excessive abandonment anxiety. They are capable of being alone, without their solitude seeming to deprive them of creativity and productivity. The Other is not essentially a menace nor does he seem like the ultimate, perfectly secure refuge. The integrated representation that organizes the personality function could be expressed as follows:

> "I am safe. The Other can care for me and protect me. My needs are natural, acceptable and tolerable." The Other remains there and is able to respond.

47

This basic security, the consequence of a good metabolization of the attachment process, can be observed in adults in love. In 1987, Hazan and Shaver demonstrated how one can find, in the romantic experience, the same types of attachment organization as in children.

These researchers observed that 56% of adults who responded to their survey had secure attachment styles, finding it easy to be close to others, to be dependent on the Other and to allow the Other to depend on them. They do not have a tendency to fear being abandoned or invaded and they have confidence in themselves and in the Other. What is more, they describe their romantic relationships as happy, loving, and secure. This does not mean that their romantic experience remains static. The intensity of their loving sentiments fluctuates, but they know how to re-find or re-create moments of intensity, as in the beginning of their relationship.

When these clients are questioned about their childhood, they tend to remember their parents' relationship as having been warm. Armed with these emotional resources and secure representations, these adults maintain their cohesion when they are far away from a loved one, because they know how to maintain the link in the absence of the Other. Nevertheless, when threatened, they prefer to be in close proximity to their loved one, where they know they will find comfort.

The socio-cultural context as a background for attachment

We have sketched a rough portrait of an adult with a healthy attachment style. All the same, let us remember that this "health" is also culturally defined. That which appears healthy at a particular period in time, in a particular society, can be seen differently in different eras and at different latitudes. All discussion as to the psychodynamics of attachment must take a person's socio-cultural field into account. We need to be able to see a client in the context of that field at a particular moment in their history.

It could be said that the end of the 60s marked a shift in the relationship that people had with "freedom", both in America and in Europe. Sexual freedom, the right to challenge authority, hedonism, and individualism have progressively become more or less incontestable and unavoidable values. The end of the 60s and the following decade saw Gestalt-therapy in its finest hour. Fritz Perls appeared on the front cover of the American magazine *Life*. Among the anti-conformist beliefs that were announced at the time, there is one that Gestaltists know well.

> I do my thing and you do your thing.
> I am not in this world to live up to your expectations,
> And you are not in this world to live up to mine,
> You are you and I am I …
> And if by chance, we find each other
> it's Beautiful.
> If not, it can't be helped (Perls, 1969).

These words are not exactly an inspiration for attachment and engagement in the long term. They seem to show the relationship and the link between two people as the result of an accident.

Society has never known a time when so many people live alone or choose not to have children, or have "temporary" conjugal relationships. The humanistic psychology of the 60s contributed to freeing human consciousness from taboos and oppressive traditions. All the same, it has probably played a role in the development of a socio-cultural context where the "temporary" seems to rule. It is probable that the children who have grown up since the 1970s have known more parental figures than any other generation. Attachment as a pathology: what do we mean by "pathological attachment"?

Attachment pathologies are the persistent and recurrent pathodynamics in a variety of contexts, with a greater preponderance in intimate relationships. They are characterized by an incapacity to make stable, interdependent connections, or alternatively by a tendency either to over-attach or, perversely, to exploit the Other through the attachment.

Two main types of attachment pathology can be recognized: the schizoid-avoidant and the anxious-ambivalent (Johnson, 1994).

Organization of the schizoid-avoidant type

In Hazan's and Shaver's study (1987), avoidant adults represented 25% of those that responded. These subjects feel a certain discomfort when in proximity to the Other. They find it difficult to have complete confidence in the Other and do not like being dependent on him/her. In addition, they are uncomfortable when somebody wants to approach them. They get the impression that the Other wants to be closer to them than they themselves want to be. Paradoxically, despite a tendency to be detached from their emotions and from relationship, they are somewhat jealous, whilst at the same time fearing intimacy. Their love life is often made up of a feeling of "being struck by lightning", followed by a retreat when they realize that their ideal love cannot exist in reality. They, therefore, rarely find what they call "true love". Finally, when they are questioned about the relationships that their parents had, they describe their mother as cold and rejecting.

Organization of the anxious-ambivalent type

In this same research (Hazan & Shaver, 1987) 19% of adults presented as anxious-ambivalent. In contrast to those with a schizoid-avoidant attachment style these had a tendency to believe that others refuse intimacy. They believe that their partner does not really love them or does not want to live with them. They seek fusion, even though they might recognize that this can scare or keep the Other away. Their relationship, as much with themselves as with the Other, is anxious, ambivalent, or fearful. They are jealous, intense, and obsessed. In contrast to the schizoid-avoidant type, there is a tendency for the father to be perceived as the significant though deceiving and unfair parent.

Seven axes of clinical presentation linked to the attachment process

We are now going to look at a set of preliminary signs of attachment problems in the very young child. From different sets of behaviour studied in children, we will attempt to formulate some hypotheses as to the form that these same sets of behaviour will take in adulthood.

Showing affection

The capacity to feel a warm experience and to express it to the Other is one of the central elements of attachment. In the child or infant, one can observe two types of distortion. The first consists of a lack of warmth or affectionate interaction with the mother. In the second, the child expresses undifferentiated warmth towards unfamiliar adults. These types of behaviour are the precursors of an attachment problem.

Certain adults seem incapable of manifesting any kind of warmth. Always reserved, they choose solitary activities. Others, on the other hand, can be excessively and prematurely warm towards people that they hardly know. The latter behaviour is typical of certain histrionic personalities and could be the result of an attachment problem defined by the inability to selectively differentiate significant from non-significant others in the environment.

Seeking comfort

The ability to seek comfort when one is in difficulty or in distress is an important indicator of the capacity for attachment. When they are in difficulty, some children do not know how to turn to an adult to find comfort. In contrast, others seek out comfort in a surprising or ambivalent way. They might "throw" themselves at anybody or ask for comfort for pain that they do not really feel physically. In extreme cases they can ask that one looks after a friend whilst in fact it is they who hurt. In a word, they present with aberrations in the capacity to seek out help.

We all know adults that have a tendency to isolate themselves when they are suffering or in difficulty. The worse they are, the less we see of them, as if they feel unpresentable. They seem to have constructed their relational capacities on a base of wounds and fundamental structural faults. The space where they have learnt to be in relationship with the Other is a few floors above their wound. When they suffer, they seem to descend into an almost object-less universe, a universe with no possibility of relating.

Others seek comfort in a roundabout way or by projective identification. Some might even go so far as to hurt someone that they love in order to be able to console them afterwards. One sees them worry the Other in order to then turn around and reassure them. One hears them saying terrible things to the loved one, and then turning around and cajoling them like a baby. One can consider this process to be an example of projective identification. When the person is in difficulty, he puts the Other in an analogous and heightened difficulty. Then, he takes care of the Other and through doing this, he cares for himself. This position recalls Klein's paranoid-schizoid position (1946). It is possible that variations of this process are at the root of the motivation for some to practise the work of the psychotherapist. Our job is one that attracts the sort of people who are profoundly hurt in the attachment area, who doubt or fear the permanence of connection. Practising as a psychotherapist, week in week out with a practice full of people who have a need for us to be there for them could mean that we have no need to cultivate connection elsewhere. And there is always someone who is worse off than us to console!

This is not a matter for cynicism. Therapists that carry this sort of wound can do their job ethically as long as they have undertaken a substantial amount of psychotherapy at the beginning of their practice. When this is the case, they have a better understanding of the why and how of the process through which they can place themselves in a position to be desired as the Other, good and caring. Their practice, then, remains on track. It could even be said that they have an advantage because they have first-hand experience of attachment injuries.

The behaviour towards support

In children in difficulty, one can observe either an excessive dependence on the Other for support, or evidence of not looking for or not using the support of the Other. Very young children, at the toddling or crawling age, are constantly looking for their mother. If she helps the child to take his first steps when he falls he does not pick himself up. Put back on his feet, if the mother (or any other person) holds out their hands, he lets himself fall down again. The child's behaviour communicates to the Other, "Don't go away, I can't stay up without you." All these behaviours are structured and organized in order to keep the Other at close range.

Inversely and particularly with those whose motor development has been faster than their emotional development, we see children that explore the universe without using available parental support. They are physically capable of climbing on anything, but do not seem to have reached the ability to anticipate and to fear.

In certain adults, we can observe more or less the same phenomena. They manifest an excessive dependence on the support of the Other. For example, certain clients play out with us a transference-countertransference situation in which the role of excellent therapist is projected on to us. However, these "excellent" clients do not function well when outside the therapy room. If we do not pay attention, we find ourselves in the absurd situation where the "excellent therapist" that we are is incapable of helping the patient to make progress where it counts. When the transferential relationship is massively positive, where we are the object of fusion, and the client does not become more autonomous outside therapy, we should consider this phenomenon to be one of the signs of a pathological attachment style.

Inversely, certain adults neither look for nor really use the support of other people. They rarely consult a therapist, unless their suffering becomes too intense and their anxiety too pronounced. When they finally do decide to consult a therapist, they can appear to make huge efforts to get a place in therapy, often accepting a place on a long waiting list. Then, when the moment comes for the therapy to begin, they cannot really say why they are there. In the long term they also cannot quite see what has changed; they can only feel it or say it when they are certain that a connection with the therapist has been established. Perversely, when connection *is* established, they are likely to induce a feeling of uselessness in the therapist who must nevertheless see this as a countertransferential indication of an attachment problem and hang in there.

The behaviour of cooperation

In the child and the infant who has a deficient attachment, one can sometimes note an absence of cooperation with the adult in charge. The child resists any injunctions and any demands and he ignores the authority figure.

In the second mode of cooperation, the infant can be extremely demanding. If for example we ask him/her to do a drawing:

> "Which crayon do you want me to use?"
> "Use whichever one you want!"
> "Should I do a big drawing or a small one?"
> "Do whatever you like!"

The infant then turns to look at other children's drawings, to see what they are doing. The result? We cannot leave him/her. One must always be there to look after and coax him.

Compulsive obedience is the third configuration. It suffices for an adult to say something for it to be done instantly. Obedience serves the function of stopping the adult mobilizing his adult forces. "If I always say yes, you will never raise your voice, you will never tell me off." By compulsively obeying, the child believes that he can neutralize the presence of the adult and therefore remains without a holding structure.

Certain clients behave in more or less the same way. Totally and prematurely consenting, they squeeze out all possibility of a disagreement or a confrontation, all possibility of a dynamic meeting.

Explorative behaviour

Certain children presenting attachment problems do not stay in contact with the adult in charge if they find themselves in an unfamiliar environment. They go off without asking. Others will prefer to engage in limited exploration because they refuse to stray too far from the mother. If she is present and we ask the child to go and play in the sandpit or in a play room, they refuse to leave the mother. They do not want to leave mummy because they have not yet acquired the certainty that they will find her again. In certain antisocial adults, one observes an insensitivity to dangers and a tendency to take risks. Similarly, those who have an avoidant personality and those who suffer from social phobia and agoraphobia sometimes have an early attachment problem.

Control behaviour

Some young children seem to want to exercise an excessive and punitive style of control. These are authoritative, almost tyrannical children. The Object or the Other must not escape from their control. A major abandonment anxiety can be hidden behind this apparent sadism.

Others establish their connections to the adult on the basis of a constant over-empathy that takes the form of excessive and inappropriate worrying or caring for the Other. At a very young age these children become the parents of their parents. This is a difficulty often occurring in the oldest female child of a large family, who lost her childhood very early. This said, the chapter on pathologies of eroticism will demonstrate that there are perhaps other factors that are involved. Effectively, that the oldest girl becomes the parent of the two parents is one thing. However, she sometimes becomes the mother of her mother and the partner of her father, and that is something else!

Obviously, certain adults exercise an excessive and punitive control over the Other. The Other cannot escape from their control. These adults can be extremely punitive or exercise their control by an "imprisoning solitude in which all the needs of the Other are anticipated, decoded, and satisfied before they have even had a chance to emerge.

The "strange situation"

The "strange situation" experiment (Ainsworth et al., 1978) was devised to study attachment patterns of very young children. The mother is asked to leave the room and a person that the child does not know is asked to enter. The reactions of the child are observed. Then the stranger leaves and the mother re-enters the room. The observers can then see how the child reconnects with the mother. In Ainsworth's original experiment infants who were securely attached played and explored the room contentedly in her presence, became appropriately anxious when left alone with a stranger and sought and received comfort when mother returned. In those children that present an attachment problem, two types of behaviour can be observed. In one case, the child did not appear to mind that the mother left the room and did not seek comfort from her when she returned. These children were called "anxious/avoidant". Another group of infants, termed "anxious/resistant", were seen to be highly distressed by mother's absence but did not seek, and even angrily rejected, comfort on her return. In the first case, one can infer that the connection is very fragile and that even a brief absence is sufficient to break the child's internal representation of mother. In the second case, one can deduce that the connection is fragile but less so than in the first case. In fact it is a very ambivalent connection. Mother's absence is experienced as a punishment and she is punished in return.

We all know someone who has a tendency to seem sulky after a physical or psychological separation. Therapists often encounter this sort of behaviour in clients after a holiday break. The client is colder, more distant. He is sulking, he is not particularly interested. Whatever connection there was before the break seems no longer to exist for him. We also know clients who claim not to have been in the least bothered or inconvenienced by our absence. When that is the case it may be an indication that the therapist does not figure at all in the client's internal world.

An attachment theory

Through this brief look at the phenomenology of attachment pathologies we can see how the behaviour of the pathological adult is often calibrated to obtain exactly the opposite of what he seems to desire. What is in the foreground is rarely a complete reflection of the investment in the object relation that has remained in the background. The two pathological profiles (Johnson, 1994; Ainsworth et al., 1978), when viewed on the seven axes outlined above, allow the clinician to begin to diagnose pathologies that are due to a developmental arrest.

The developmental theories that we glanced over in the previous chapter show how a secure attachment is the result of a fundamental and interactive process between the organism and the environment. For Klein, a secure attachment can only be established with the achievement of the depressive position, while for Mahler, it is the result of a progression through the stages that lead to separation—individuation. Winnicott considers that attachment is linked, in the first instance, to mother's capacity for empathy, followed by a careful and progressive distancing that allows the child to be creative when "alone in the presence of another". For Fairbairn, secure attachment is the result of mature dependence.

The psychoanalytic developmental tradition proposes that a secure attachment only occurs if a strong connection is initially generated and that it is this connection that permits the differentiation between the Self and the Other. In the long term, a significant connection remains, constituting identity and the Self. Klein's depressive position includes an empathic consideration for the Object, and Fairbairn's maturity retains a kind of "dependence". Finally, for Freud and the drive tradition, attachment is achieved through a lengthy process of the satisfaction of needs or impulses that finishes with the internalization of parental figures into the ego ideal and the super-ego.

We will now look at the specific contribution of Bowlby (1969), whose work bridges the gap between psychoanalysis and ethology, which is the scientific study of animal behaviours.

Bowlby's contribution

For Bowlby, the need for human contact is not learned but is innate and permanent. Paradoxically, he sees our inbuilt need for attachment as supporting autonomy. One cannot go off and explore the richness of the world unless one is secure in the connection with the Other and believes that the Other will not disappear in their absence.

Two types of research gave Bowlby food for thought. The first was the work of Rene Spitz (1945) on the effects of early maternal deprivation. Spitz was one of the first to use child observation as a research tool in the area of maternal deprivation. Spitz discovered through observing children in hospital that simply responding to their hunger and other physical needs was not sufficient to construct object relations.

Bowlby was also influenced by the work of Harlow and Suomi (1971) as to ethological perspective. Ethological observation finds that infants from other species respond like humans to the presence or absence of the mother. Through studying the developmental stages of certain animal species, one learns that in adult life the consequences of developmental failures are not exclusive to human beings. For example, in certain canary species that develop in an environment that provides fledglings no material instruction in nest-building in adulthood, these same canaries do not use optimal nest-building material even if it is made available to them.

According to the observations of Harlow and Suomi and several other researchers from the ethological perspective, animals are naturally supplied with behavioural systems that allow the immediate establishment of a relationship with a fellow being. It is to Harlow and Suomi that we owe the research that taught us that Rhesus monkeys prefer to attach themselves to a "mother" made of terrycloth even if she does not give milk, than to a milk-giving mother made out of wire (Harlow & Suomi, 1971).

Bowlby came to believe that the interactive and emotional needs of the infant precede and are primary to his experience of maternal caring. As Zazzo (1979) has written: "The construction of the first bonds between the mother (or primary carer) and the infant respond to a fundamental biological need, meaning that it is not a derivative of anything else" (p. 102).

Studies in infant observation support this point of view. At birth, the infant can distinguish the mother's voice from others reading the same text (Fifer & DeCasper, 1980). Already at one week old, it is capable of discriminating between a passage heard *in utero* and a control text (ibid.). Very early on, the infant's vision focuses at a distance of 20 centimetres from a figure, the typical distance between him/herself and the face of his breastfeeding mother (Stern, 1977). At one week, he/she recognizes the mother enough to be troubled if she wears a mask, or if, for example, the infant hears the voice of another person while the mother is present (Tronick & Adamson, 1980).

For Bowlby, the human infant has ways of attracting the attention of the parent whose response is also intuitive and inborn. Attachment bonds are the result of a system and not of an individual. This is a perspective that is compatible with both field theory (Lewin, 1951) and Winnicott's concept of the "nursing couple". From this we might draw the conclusion that if attachment to the mother is crucial, support for that needs to include other figures in the wider field, such as the father, siblings, and the baby sitter.

A synthesis that is useful for contemporary clinical practice: from the theoretical background to the appreciation of risk and resilience factors

The organism: risk factors

If we admit the validity of the work which claims that genetic heritage (temperament) plays a role in the development of personality (Cloninger, Svrakic & Przybeck, 2000), it seems logical that a child who has inherited a difficult temperament will be at greater risk in developing a capacity for a secure attachment. What does one mean by "difficult temperament"? Current research is not precise about this. Nevertheless it is reasonable to assume that the less the temperament of the child is compatible with that of its parents or primary caretakers the greater the risk. It has been established (Breslau et al., 1996; Cox, Hopkins & Hans, 2000) that there is a higher incidence of attachment pathologies in people who were born prematurely. This might be because the neurological immaturity of these infants lasts longer. Physical pains (ear infections, colic, etc.) may also be considered to be a risk factor in that they probably disturb early on in the baby's life the possibility of feeling secure. A Kleinian might say that these infants phantasize that the pain is a form of internal persecution. If the mother is unable to resolve the baby's pain, regardless of her competence or her real empathy, she cannot be firmly represented as the "good Other", capable of protecting and containing. Other risk factors include separation due to the illness or incarceration of the mother, neurological, physical, or learning difficulties, and fœtal alcohol syndrome.

The organism: resilience factors?

The logic of this model is based on the supposition that there is a certain temperamental configuration which disposes one to surmount unfavourable developmental conditions. Does this configuration really exist? Apparently it does. Has it been observed, measured, or demonstrated? No, but in general a temperament characterized by a sensitivity to reward and a high level of persistence is under-represented in people that present with personality disorders (Sadock & Sadock, 2000).

The family environment: risk factors

It is obvious that we should look first to the family environment for the main cause of attachment pathologies. The psychoanalytic tradition abounds with causal hypotheses on the subject. Today, clinical research allows us to appreciate the level of impact of the relationship between certain factors and the prevalence of specific pathologies. We know, for example, that more attachment pathologies are found among those who had teenage parents or those whose parents were drug addicts (Levy, Orlans & Winger, 1999).

However, the most consistently correlated factor in attachment pathologies is the absence of the maternal figure. Whether this absence is due to a hospitalization, an imprisonment, or a prolonged disappearance, the effects on early development are manifest. In the most serious cases the child completely detaches from the maternal figure (Bowlby, 1973). In addition, during the period of absence, the mother's feelings towards the child can change (Bensel & Paxson, 1979; Leiderman & Seashore, 1975; Peterson & Mehl, 1978; Heinicke & Westheimer, 1966). The family can also reorganize itself, excluding—at least emotionally—the child.

A mother who suffers from post-natal or other forms of depression will have a negative effect on her baby by non-verbally communicating her morbid thoughts: "I am not a good mother", "The child is abnormal", "He would be better off without me" (Kissane & Ball, 1988). A depressed mother is less interactive with her baby, less capable of caring for it (Cohn, Campbell, Matias & Hopkins, 1990). Post- partum depression is particularly problematic for the newborn child in that it is directly related to the birth of the baby and can result in an inability to love it. In certain serious cases of post-natal depression mothers have homicidal thoughts about killing their baby (Sneddon, Kerry & Bant, 1981). These mothers have great difficulty in being maternal and come to believe that their child is too difficult, that he is uncontrollable or mentally stronger than themselves (Uddenberg & Englesson, 1978).

In the case of severe or persistent mental disorders, whether they be of a biological or psychological origin, one often sees aberrant attitudes appear towards maternity (Jacobsen & Miller, 1999). Psychotic parents often lack the capacity to understand an infant's non-verbal clues. They touch and play less with the child. Antipsychotic drugs can also reduce the capacity for good enough parenting.

It is important, however, not to draw hasty conclusions. The universe of family risk factors is complex and involves many elements. There are also other influences on the capacity for maternal caring in the pathological mother. Among these are her own experiences of being cared for as a child (Main & Hesse, 1990), her age, the number of children that she has had, her relationship with her partner, financial resources, a capacity for insight, her response to treatment (Cassell & Coleman, 1995) and available social support (Crittenden, 1985; Fendrich, Weissman & Warner, 1990).

All these forces act in a complex, dynamic field. A depressed mother who is well supported, correctly treated and who does not have financial problems, will obviously be less pathological than an isolated, single mother who lives in a state of serious material deprivation.

We are also becoming more and more interested in the intergenerational aspects of attachment. Those parents who themselves have severe attachment problems tend to abandon, mistreat, or abuse their children. In 80% of cases, those families at high risk provoke severe attachment problems in their children (Levy, Orlans & Winger, 1999). In addition the children of chronically depressed mothers begin very early in life to parent their mother and their brothers and sisters (Zeanah & Klitzke, 1991).

The family environment: resilience factors

Cyrulnik, a French ethologist believes (2000) that the preventative or corrective effect of what he calls "affective mentors" has been underestimated. He looked at the factors that influence why some children are damaged by their difficult childhoods, while others grow up into secure, creative, and loving adults? Cyrulnik describes the ingredients of resilience, the ability to heal childhood wounds and to move on, making sense of what happened in the past and forming better emotional and social bonds. He believes that the need for affection is so strong that even those who seem completely deprived of it will attach themselves to anything that holds out hope, at whatever cost. He has seen in his extensive contact with troubled children that the simple fact of having someone—a teacher, a neighbour, the plumber—with whom to exchange even two or three ordinary sentences, can have a positive impact.

The social environment: risk factors

The family system does not exist in a vacuum. The socio-political and cultural environment also influences the quality of early bonding and the establishment of a secure attachment. Poverty, geographic isolation, and social exclusion have a significant impact on the development of attachment bonds. So does a child being the victim of or witnessing violence or abuse outside the family environment. We can understand better, for example, the detrimental effects of placing a child in foster care, particularly when he is moved from one foster family or care home to another. A child that is taken away from his family has greater needs for stability and consistency. If he is in the charge of multiple carers, any beneficial effects that might have resulted from being removed from his family of origin may be lost.

When the attachment period has been affected by a preponderance of risk factors, the pathological consequences in adulthood are multiple and are not limited to DSM Axis II personality disorders, even though these criteria represent many of the unconscious reproductions of contact dilemmas that interrupt development. Attachment problems can also result in Axis I disorders, such as anxiety disorders, dissociative disorders, behavioural and oppositional disorders, and attention deficit and hyperactivity disorders.

To sum up ...

Attachment is probably one of the most important primary developmental achievements. It is the source of our affective security and of our capacity for engagement. Early deregulation of attachment can interrupt the metabolism of important future developmental phases. The psychotherapist needs to take this into account. In order to do this I propose three tools. First, a decoding of the patient's presenting problems and life story using the seven axes of behaviour and attitudes relating to the problem of attachment. Second, using either Johnson's (or Ainsworth's) prototypical terminology, identifying the patient's probable developmental path towards disturbed attachment. And third, taking into consideration both the risk and resilience factors in the wider field that may have played a part in the elaboration and metabolizing of attachment.

A psychotherapist who uses this three pronged approach might, for example, observe that a patient seems to have pathological predispositions in a majority of the seven axes of behaviour. Reflective and focused attention to the client's presentation and to the transference-countertransference dimension will aid in arriving at a diagnosis of either predominantly schizoid-avoidant or anxious-ambivalent organization. Finally, dialogic work in field 4, the developmental past, will support an active investigation of the developmental field configuration, thereby revealing the unique relationship between risk factors and resilience factors.

If, at the end of this clinical and reflexive stance, the therapist concludes that there is a weakness in the metabolism of attachment bonding, it will be necessary to calibrate interventions and to manage repetitions as they emerge in the transferential field in a manner that allows for the construction of the meaning and ultimately the reactivation in the clinical situation of damaged developmental processes. It is this rich and complex process that we will discuss in the next chapter.

CHAPTER FIVE

Treating attachment issues

Relational psychotherapy, with its roots in both Gestalt-therapy and object relations theory, essentially sees treat-ment of attachment issues as a reactivation and resolution of developmental processes. This reactivation has been shown to be fundamental in the treatment of attachment disorders. This is why it is necessary to identify the client's relational issues outside the therapy room because they carry the imprints of the devel-opmental issues that were not resolved at the attachment stage. In addition, it is necessary to reactivate these issues within the framework of the therapeutic work. This means that the therapeu-tic relationship, before it can be a reparative space, must be a space for reconstruction and attempting to make sense of what is unre-solved. Levy, Orlans, and Winger (1999) describe this process as: revisit, revise, revitalize. In order for the therapist to be able to do this he must develop and maintain three fundamental competen-cies: reflexive competency, affective competency, and interactive competency.

Reflexive competence

Maintaining a stable therapeutic frame is essential in the treatment of early developmental issues. Effectively, in the absence of this framework, the therapy will be limited to superficial adjustments. Stability and structure support the therapist to focus his attention, which encourages empathic resonance. The therapist must recognize the attachment issues that lie behind a patient's symptoms, often appearing to be something else. Attachment issues can, for example, be hidden behind the narcissistic False Self. Understanding these issues constitutes a major part of the treatment. The therapist must also know how to evaluate the risk and resilience factors in field 4, but must, above all, be attentive to tracking all reproductions of attachment dilemmas, in fields 1, 2, and 3. Finally, attention to the transference/countertransference dynamic is crucial in understanding what is brought to the therapy but remains unsaid.

Affective competence

The intimacy that is required for effective therapeutic work around attachment exposes the therapist to a relationship with others whose relational capacity has never fully developed. These clients sometimes present very challenging relational dysfunctions that can be heavy to carry in the therapeutic context. They are either cold, critical, and discouraging, or appear to be driven by a desire for fusion with the therapist. In either case the therapist's capacity for acceptance and engagement can be sorely tried. This is why, even when the client is not lovable, the capacity to love the client or at least generate a positive affect constitutes the foundation of the work. In order to mobilize these emotions, the therapist must sometimes overcome a quite natural reticence to certain types of patients: those who do not trust and do not know how to make a stable link, those who have a great need to control defensively, not sadistically, and those who fear rapprochement and lack the capacity for reciprocity. The therapist will need to visit and revisit his own attachment issues that lie behind the surface of his own personality adjustments.

Interactive competence

Treating attachment issues is probably the prototype of a relational psychotherapy. Here the therapist is called upon to "make sense" of often preverbal experiences and to help the client to put these into words. The level of the dialogue must, therefore, be adjusted in order to allow the client to access the depths of archaic experiences. The therapist who insists on using a more formalized language style may well impede or slow down access to "unresolved situations". What is more, given that clients will be encouraged and supported to "grow up" in the process of the therapy, the therapist must adjust the nature of his interactions with them. A six-month-old baby does not interact in the same way as a six-year-old or a 16-year-old. The therapist must be able to adjust the level of his language adequately to his experience of the client at each point in time. Finally, because the work around attachment issues must often allow the exploration of preverbal issues, the therapist must consider whether touch is appropriate in such cases. Since the work of Bowlby and Winnicott, we understand the importance of touch and of physical contact as one of the basic modes of relating. Not only does physical contact transmit secure "holding", but it also activates neurological functions in the central nervous system that control attachment behaviours (Schore, 1994).

How might it be possible then, to incorporate, in a dialogical therapy, the possibility of touch in the Winnicottian sense of "holding"? A well attuned touch intervention can induce certain regressive states that activate cellular and bodily memories and that mobilize attachment behaviours. Obviously there exist practitioners in psychosomatic therapies such as bio-energetics and integrated body psychotherapy for whom these intervention techniques are familiar. For psychotherapists from other traditions it can be difficult and complex in a dialogical practice to use touch. Touch can have many different meanings and take many different forms, from the most well conceived and attuned to complete therapeutic failure. Sometimes it can be acting out on the therapist's part. Nevertheless, in order to understand and treat attachment issues, it is necessary to consider using touch. At the heart of dialogical work, each therapist must find their comfort zone with using touch. No therapist should work lightly with this powerful tool. However, no one should dismiss the possibility of using touch because it is proscribed by ethical codes. Having said that, the therapist needs to work ethically within the limits of his competence and, in some areas, further training in the therapeutic use of touch may be required.

Consider this as an example of an effective intervention using touch. A young woman came to her therapy session with a children's book and, in a creative adjustment, she asked her therapist to read her a story. The therapist agreed. However, the latter part of the interview shows that it was therapeutically indicated that she lean her back on the therapist while listening to the story, and thereby let herself be "carried". It was not possible for her to be sitting in her chair while someone read her a story. That would not have made any sense. This body to body contact revealed itself, through the dialogue, to be essential.

Luce: a clinical vignette

Before going any further in the discussion of treatment, let us have a look at the first few minutes of a first session with a client who was referred by her GP for symptoms that seemed to correspond to adaptive difficulties with a depressed mood. We will continue to refer to this piece of work throughout the chapter.

Th1:   Good morning Luce, what can I do for you?

C1:   It's my doctor who suggested that I see someone .... At the moment things are quite difficult ... I ... well, I don't feel good talking about it. It's my friend, well my boyfriend, I don't know if it's that, but for the last two weeks I really don't feel well. I'm having a lot of trouble sleeping, nothing interests me any more. I hardly eat anything. So much that sometimes I actually feel like fainting, as if I'm going to black out.

Th2:   Hmm. It seems difficult even talking about it? What did your doctor say about your dizzy spells?

C2:   Apparently it's not physical ....

Th3:   Early on you started talking about your boyfriend ... what's going on with him?

C3:   We're no longer together ....

Th4:   Is that difficult for you? What happened?

C4:   I don't know. I don't understand it. Everything was going all right and then, all of a sudden, he had someone else. He said he wanted to have a bit of space; he didn't want to commit to a relationship ....

Th5:   Is it hard to talk about it? Do you love him?

C5:   It's weird because, in fact I'm not even sure if I do love him. I thought he loved me. I was surprised to react like that. It's not the end of the world ... but it's as if I am disoriented. It's crazy, even if he wanted to get back together I don't think I would want to. So why am I like this? Am I going mad?

Th6:   You don't seem mad to me, as you say. But you are surely suffering and I would say a bit lost. As if the experience of losing is more important, at this moment, than what you have lost ....

C6:   Why do I feel so bad, why does it hurt so much?

Th7:   We are going to try and see a bit more clearly together .... Something important seems to have been touched on by this break-up. Could you tell me a bit about the history of your relationship with this man? What is his name?

C7:   Marc. He's a strange guy. Sort of actor on the dole type. I met him at some friends of my sister's .... He made me laugh ... [cries]. He was funny and he flirted with me. Once I asked his age. He told me that he was ten minutes old. He was born when I smiled at him [emotion, tears].

Th8:   That's a whole declaration. That's quite a line ....

C8:   He was very good at that ....

Th9:   You're angry huh?

C9:   Me, I thought it was true. Idiot. Any old idiot would have known that it was just the words of a charmer, repeated 1000 times in sleazy bars.

Th11:   Angry at him and ... yourself?

C11:   I'm mad at myself to have been had like that. You'd think I don't know how to live, that I don't know anything about life.

Th12:   Perhaps yourself, you are ... younger than you thought.

C12:   [Cries.] I don't know any more. I feel old.

Th13:   How old are you Luce?

C13:   I'd like to say ten minutes. But no, I'm 35 years old, even if today I feel like I'm 50.

Th14:   So you met Marc, he touched you, and you were together for, what, 18 months? What was it like to live together for that year and a half?

C14:   Well, I don't know if you could call that living together as a couple. We saw each other but we weren't living together. [Silence …] I live with my parents ….

Th15:   You seem a bit embarrassed to say that ….

C15:   In fact what I mean is that I live in a flat that they did up for me.

Th16:   Am I right in believing that you are a bit embarrassed by that, that you live in the same house as them?

C16:   But it's not their house! It's an arrangement that suits everyone. As I work for my father and the office is in the house, it's far more convenient like that: I don't have to do long journeys each morning and evening. My place is my place!

Th17:   …

C17:   It's true that that bothers me a bit because I know well enough that it seems a bit like a baby holding on to its mother's skirts. God knows that my mother's skirts …

Th18:   You want to tell me about your mother?

C18:   Not really.

Th19:   …

C19:   If it was her, I'd be somewhere else.

Th20:   It seems like a difficult relationship ….

C20:   Bah, I don't know if one can even call it a relationship. My mother is in a relationship only with herself. And even then …

Th21:   You seem angry when you talk about her … or disappointed?

C21:   It's not about my mother …. I don't know what it is.

Th22:   You seem sad now.

C22:   I don't like talking about her.

Th23:   Talking about her, it's a bit like making her exist? … Giving her life?

C23:   … [Cries]

Th24:   Did she give you life?

C24:   The minimum. A packet of cold meat, came out of a packet of cold meat!

Th25:   How that must be painful, to have to say that …

C25:   … [Cries]

Th26:   Since you came in here, I feel as though I'm with a young woman who is hurting a lot. But I don't feel cold with you.

C26:   Marc said I was refreshing like the sunshine.

Th27:   He had a feeling for the … and the contrast.

C27:   …

Th28:   Like in our exchange up to now. We are in a contrast. The part where you were with Marc, gave life, light, was warm. That part where you describe, in relation to your mother has something a bit … like it's a bit exaggerated said like that but …

C28:   It's not exaggerated. It's that. She never wanted me to live.

Th29:   And … have you lived?

C29:   Until I met Marc, perhaps not. I was perhaps better off like that ….

Th30:   You've become angry with yourself again. That seems to happen when you speak of your relationships. At the same time you seem to say something true for yourself, when you speak of not much life in your life.

C30:   35 years old, no boyfriend, lives with her parents, works for her father.

Th31:   You have to pitch it like that in order to be able to say it, huh? Like a failure?

C31:   I've studied, I went to university in England, and I've lived. But it's like that inside, at the heart, I am … not even a child.

Th32:   An embryo?

C32:   … [Silence, tears]

Th33:   …

C33:   You know what my mother did, when she knew she was pregnant with me?

Th34:   …

C35:   She went off on a journey to South America, rucksack and all!

Th36:   And what sense do you make of that, today?

C36:   She wanted to get rid of me, have a miscarriage!

Th37:   But you hung on …

C37:   … [Tears]

Th38:   Perhaps you are still, in a way …

C38:   You're hard … but you're right.

Th39:   That's the first time you have spoken about me.
C39:   I'm afraid that I've hurt you by saying that.
Th40:   ... It's as if a third relationship has just been born.
C40:   What do you mean?
Th41:   You and Marc, you and your mother and now you and me.
C41:   You're not like my mother.
Th42:   After what you've just said, that seems like a compliment ...
C42:   [Laughs, smiles ...]
Th43:   What am I like?
C43:   I don't know ....
Th44:   I believe you. I believe that you don't yet know what sort of connection we have started to make between us ....

The specific framework for treating attachment issues

We can see in the above interview some of the characteristics that we touched on in the last chapter.

The impasses of attachment manifest themselves in different ways depending on whether the client presents a "schizoid-avoidant" or an "anxious-ambivalent" type of organization. They are particularly observed in the seven axes of attachment behaviours that we looked at in chapter Four.

As we have seen, various criteria for DSM Axis II personality disorders are closely linked to these attachment behaviours.

The work with people who present arrested development in the area of attachment needs certain signposts for each of the phases: repetition—recognition—restoration. Repetition and the transference relationship

Essentially the reactivation of attachment issues appears to modulate and colour the transference relationship. It is through the process of repetition, often through projective identifications, that the transference relationship unfolds. We can understand, then, the transference relationship as being the repetition of impasses in contact. Attachment issues, like all developmental issues, tend to repeat themselves in a more or less unconscious effort to complete or maintain themselves. Why? Because repetition is necessary for maintaining the cohesion of the Self. The person can only make sense of her experience and protect herself from the archaic suffering associated with attachment issues in this way. Like this, if a hyper-warm and overly extroverted therapist had said to Luce: "You are a very lovable person and I'm shaking with indignation at the thought that your mother could reject you like that," she would have found herself plunged into a universe where she did not understand much of what some people were talking about. On the other hand the therapist in the vignette limited herself to saying, at Th26: "I feel as though I am with a young woman who is hurting a lot. But I don't feel cold with you." This minimally reparative intervention helped to establish a therapeutic alliance, which we can see happening at the end of the extract.

Perhaps somewhat perversely in order to make sense of an unhappy life the client may need things to happen more or less as they have always happened. They actually have a need to be in danger or in isolation. It is as though their suffering gives meaning to their life and must be clung to. However, at the same time they also need to be relieved of it. Needing on the one hand to stay the same they also hope for transformation and live their lives in that ambivalence alternating between states of repair and relapse. In fact relapse is likely to follow a therapeutic reparation We can understand this if we see it as an attempt at self-protection, not therapeutic sabotage, because as long as they can replay these impasses on the surface, they will not find the original archaic wound.

Attachment issues that were not resolved at crucial phases of development seek to complete themselves, especially in the framework of three types of significant relationships in field 3: the romantic relationship, close friendships, and the parent-child relationships when the client is the parent. Those persons that are deprived on the attachment side often relive their own infantile wounds when they have children of their own. Sometimes, they repair themselves by succeeding in giving that which they were deprived of. They would therefore say, with emotion, that they are conscious that the child they are caring for could be themselves. "The things that I do for him, nobody ever did for me and it does me good to do this for someone else." However, for this experience to be accessible to consciousness, the person must have done a certain amount of the work of elaboration and recognition. When that is not the case, in general there is a sort of blindness to the issue. There may even be an unconscious but intentional need to withhold: "I can't give my child what I didn't get," often with the rationalization that one cannot give what one has never received.

The repetitions that undermine the client's experience and that bring them to therapy are elaborated in field 3, that of significant relationships in the present. They are illustrated by the clinical phenomenology described in chapter Five. All the same, these issues also reproduce themselves in the context of the therapeutic relationship (fields 1 and 2). The intimacy and the implicit boundaries or frame of the therapeutic relationship are combined to evoke and to reactivate developmental episodes or phases, for the therapeutic relationship is not like an ordinary relationship. For therapists, who are daily exposed to this world, it is easy to lose sight of the unusual nature of this type of relationship.

For the client, it is also out of the ordinary: meeting at a fixed time with a complete stranger and revealing the most intimate secrets in the assurance of perfect confidentiality and the likelihood of receiving an empathic welcome. This is a truly unique experience. Effectively, the therapist accepts a contract to reconstruct the client's developmental path. We care, we inspire and frustrate, we also become the parental figure. The client comes to tell us all about it, saying in a way, "Look, Daddy, how I've grown up"; "Look, Mummy, I fell over and my knee is bleeding!"; "Look, Daddy, how useless you are: the advice you gave me really put me in the shit!". The therapist, in the parental function, must practise the handling as well as the "holding" in the Winnicottian sense of the term.

What's more, working one to one with the client, in intimacy and over a long time, the therapist can also take on the role of a partner in a couple. A fantasy of a couple is present in the therapist's consulting room regardless of the "sex" of each of the partners in the therapeutic relationship. In brief, the therapeutic structure is one of the most fertile places for the reactivation of developmental issues of attachment. Now let us look at the two prototypes of repetition: the schizoid-avoidant type and the anxious-ambivalent type.

The repetitions of the schizoid-avoidant style at the heart of the therapeutic relationship

In order not to weigh down the text by repeated warnings, let us specify it here, once and for all, that the examination of various repetitions supposes a therapist that is conscious of his/her own attachment style and issues. That is the essence of affective competency. This is never to be taken for granted and is characterized by a constant questioning of emotions and thoughts that emerge in the clinical situation.

One of the most obvious repetitions of the schizoid-avoidant client comes from the necessity, for this type of client, to isolate or suppress affect. In the therapist, this isolation or suppression of affect provokes a projective identification. Through this complex and unconscious operation, the therapist can come to feel distant and to intellectualize. When one feels like this (distant and intellectualizing) one may understand that a projective identification (PI) is the cause. In effect, the client does not want to feel what he should be feeling, so he works in a way to get us to feel it. The therapist thereby becomes situationally "schizoid"! This is a case of concordant projective identification. And in addition, if the therapist seeks to defend himself too much against this PI, he can become too affectionate, which results in the heightening of the associative defence. The client entered cold, the therapist received the first signs of projective identification and became anxious. Not wanting to fall into his own coldness, he counteracts the movement by its contrast. While the therapist attempts to "warm himself up" the client is "freezing". This is a case of complementary PI.

The therapist can also get impatient if he (or she, of course) underestimates the size of the terror that the defence is covering. He might want to confront the client's resistance at its affective emergence, which would, most of the time, be ill advised. Effectively, on the surface of the defence there are few indications of the disorganizing terror that is behind it. The therapist has at his disposal a whole array of techniques designed to activate and heighten experience. All the same the unconsidered use of these techniques can put him in the position of the sorcerer's apprentice, capable of unblocking things without really knowing what to do with what has been unblocked. The therapist therefore finds him or herself with a client who has only two options: either keep themselves together by heightening the defence, or fragment in order to no longer feel the intensity of the affect. This is why we understand the importance of "holding", in the sense where the therapist must be able to psychologically "hold" in the adult client the deprived, unattached "baby". The therapist must know how to maintain a warm stance without losing himself in a projective identification. This warmth is a form of affective empathy that is slightly exaggerated. What the therapist may feel might be described in this way: "I am touched by the need of this child to freeze itself. I admit and I accept that." In that way the therapist can continue the dialogue slowly and gently, without seeking to heighten emotion, continuing to be present for the client. Metaphorically, the therapist becomes the mother that holds the baby and speaks gently to him, because the therapist is near to him. If not, therapists can find themselves in the position of the mother who needs to be diverted by the baby and who becomes anxious because the baby does not play with her.

In the higher functioning levels of a schizoid-avoidant organization, we often find an adequate level of social competency. However these competencies are accompanied by a lot of intellectualization and "spiritual" references. While the therapist must respect the spiritual experience of these clients, he must keep in mind that, as in every other experience, be it intellectual, sexual, or political, this spiritual experience can be used as a defence. Certain types of spirituality reveal themselves to be defensive and their psychic function is above all to place the therapist "off centre" in relation to the suffering that has its roots in an attachment wound.

Obviously, certain people in the higher levels of functioning are capable of speaking about their suffering in transcendental terms. It is down to the therapist to verify if it is an authentic experience, patiently constructed along the lines of real suffering or whether it is a schizoid defence that has conveniently taken on the appearance of a spiritual experience.

An experience that has been avoided will never really be resolved. Even if the anxiety about contact is better compensated for by these clients, it continues to be present. Their Self is experienced as damaged, tarnished, or even bad. This experience of identity often comes down, for them, to a question about their right to exist. "I was rejected or I was not connected with at my birth. I must therefore have something damaged in me, something not right, because even my mother did not accept me. Therefore I am bad. So do I have the right to exist?" When Luce says, "She didn't want me to live," she is expressing this question through a projective mechanism.

This lack of the right to existence can convert itself into a projective identification through which the therapist becomes the container and feels the client's experience. So what happens in this case? One can feel the emergence of an experience resembling disapprobation, of condemnation, or even a threat to the client's psychic survival. In addition, when in contact with feeling this experience emerging (disapprobation, critical condemnation of the client's way of living or not living), the therapist maybe feeling as if he wants to warn the client that behaving as they do is putting their psychic survival in peril, the therapist is giving way to a complementary projective identification on the theme "Do I or do I not have the right to exist?". In giving way, he condemns the client to a psychic death. This is sometimes the case when, for example, therapists ask themselves if they shouldn't put an end to doing therapy with this type of client, which is, from the client's point of view, the equivalent of an exile, an abortion, an execution.

A therapist who, alternatively, focuses on his emotion and who questions its meaning could notice that in fact he feels disempowered. Obviously, asking questions about whether to carry on or not is a clinical necessity, but it can also be the therapist's defence against disempowerment. In fact, the representation that was activated in the MFR (Matrix of Field Representations) of the therapist presents itself as such: "This child is psychically stillborn. I can't do anything for her therapeutically and it is not my fault."

Let us remind ourselves that these clients do not know what they feel and can seem cold or out of touch with themselves. In sessions, they carry something dead. The time stretches on and the atmosphere becomes cold and desert-like. One must understand this microclimate as resulting from a defence against a background of terror. Under this terror can be found a primitive rage and split, that through projective identification, is going to make the therapist furious. The client plays dead. He is without relational resonance, unable to acknowledge the existence of the therapist. By doing this, he does to the therapist what was done to him before. He does not acknowledge the existence of those that come into his world. In response the therapist becomes angry instead of, and in the place of, the client.

In addition, when one feels one's own anger mounting because of a lack of reciprocity, one must mobilize an interactive competency that is able to put into words some elements of this experience. In the best case, one might understand it as an experience of the client that is seeking to re-localize and to manifest itself in the therapist, in order that he can feel what it's like to be the client. Primitive rage itself underlies the terror associated with the relationship. We are in the universe of things that orbit around death anxiety: homicide, infanticide, matricide. And in this way, Luce (C24) speaks of a fantasy of infanticide and even matricide: "… cold meat, came out of a packet of cold meat". We could say that she is naming something dead in the experience that she has of herself in connection with she who had given her life.

Repetition of the anxious-ambivalent style at the heart of the therapeutic relationship

In the case of higher functioning, we find clients who are driven by an excessive need to look after others, a position that they adopted very young as children of depressive mothers. These clients, in contrast to the schizoid-avoidant client, are particularly thoughtful towards the therapist. In them we can see a compensatory function for the devotion, followed by depression and illness, as if resulting from the split in the representations of Self and representations of Object. In other words, these clients devote themselves to the Other in an excessive manner and their devotion is proportional to the fact that nobody was devoted to them. After which, they are prone to periods of depression or falling ill, as a way of punishing those who did not look after them.

There is, in this role of all-powerful parent, a sort of pretend grandiosity that one must not confuse with narcissistic grandiosity. Here, the defence is more primitive. It is nothing to do with, to employ Freudian terms, the ego ideal or with the idealized me. The objective is not to gain esteem or admiration from the other, but to ensure survival. The sense that comes out of hermeneutic dialogue is sometimes this: the child cares for the parent in order to ensure his own survival. Inversely the client can relocate his own vulnerability in the Other, and through the Other can care for himself. This process of identity confusion and the unconscious links between field 4 and field 3 often puts these clients into intimate relationships with turbulent figures, the function of which is to re-create field 4.

We can well understand how they are hard put to admit their needs. They can only exist if relocated in the Other and, again, the tool used for this relocation is projective identification. Because they cannot really admit to their motives, the therapist is made to feel as if he is not useful. From their point of view, to express their needs would be to risk feeling their archaic needs which constitute a real prelude to abandonment. They have constructed a Matrix of Field Representations (MFR) made of polarities such as weak/all-powerful, ill/carer, etc. This way of representing the universe and the direction of their lives allows them to swim on the surface of troubled waters without risking going under. In this way they reproduce impasses in contact impregnated with issues of dependence. This phenomenon appears in a therapeutic relationship that is evolving well. Clients can hereby start to feel their dependence. By complementary projective identification, the therapist himself appears and sometimes behaves as if he is an Object that is impossible to satisfy.

In these clients, the split anger often generates a generalized and dystonic irritability, a genuine rage and despair that comes from field 4: they could not count on the parental figures even though their lives literally depended on them. Recognition and the hermeneutic relationship should only be undertaken after an exploration and grounding in fields 1 and 2, in order to limit the effects of a defensive rigidity.

Let us now consider the signposts for work around recognition in attachment issues. The difficulty in this work resides in the fact that the essence of the problem is preverbal. Even if useful work is done on body process, thereby permitting access to the interrupted attachment issue, the construction of meaning still necessitates using words. For the therapist, the difficulty lies in calibrating and in choosing the level of language that will maintain the emotion, whilst opening up the possibility of an elaboration of the meaning of the work.

It remains possible that clients can experience the work around recognition as a refusal to satisfy their needs and as blame for having expressed them. When they arrive in therapy in a dried up state and "thirsty", to ask them how come they haven't already had something to drink, is like saying to them "You won't get water from me." They feel.criticised for having demands and blamed for bringing them to you.

Finally, the essence of their defences serves to neutralize the hermeneutic effort. Like anybody, they do not wish to feel the intolerable, which is why they tend to isolate emotion from thought. It is for them a protection against the terror, the anxiety of death and the rage that might become conscious and submerge them.

This is why denial and intellectualization so often come into the dialogue and devitalize it. For all these reasons (essential preverbal character of the issue, denial of needs, and defences against meaning making), they have difficulty participating fully in the hermeneutic dialogue. They have a bad memory of conflict, of events from field 4, in brief everything that may reactivate a disorganizing affect. This is why it is often preferable not to engage in the work of recognition without having had an exploration and considerable grounding in fields 1 and 2. This work should be designed so as to harness emotion, to reduce the denial of needs, thereby disarming the principal defences against the creation of meaning. This seems to be the choice made by Luce's therapist, when she opens the dialogue on the budding and unknown relationship that is beginning to be made.

Knowing the difficulties that these clients have in participating in a hermeneutic dialogue, it is often useful to offer ideas at the beginning of the session and ask questions near the end of the session. In fact at the beginning of the session we must give them more than we ask of them, like water to the thirsty. It is a case of activating the connection and verifying that this is driving them to become interested in the meaning of their experience.

Let us imagine for example that we are at the second session with Luce. The therapist could say, "We started our work last week by talking about your relationships with Marc and other people. If you remember, at the end of our session, you started to talk about you and me. Can you tell me if you have thought any more about me since last week?" Here it is a case of a rather directive opening. Luce could say, "Yes, I have thought about the things that we said and I said to myself that I liked meeting you and I hope that this week will go well." Here the therapist would not say, "How would you like it to go?" or "What do you mean by 'going'?" It is too early. According to the principle introduced above, it would be better to say "I feel confident that it will continue to go well. I saw last week that you were capable of making connections between different situations and see the resemblances. That is promising! Do you see what I mean?" At the end of the session the therapist could say, "You told me last week that your mother didn't want you to live. Why, from your own point of view? What motive could she have for not wanting to see you born?" This would be a good question at the end of the interview. It is useful for the work of internalization and meaning-making as the client will keep it in mind between the second and third meeting. It is preferable that she does not respond too quickly to this sort of question.

At the beginning of the third session, the therapist might say, "Do you remember that question that I asked you last week?" If the client does not remember, the work of internalizing needs to be done. If alternatively she remembers, the therapist could say, "Great, I'm happy to know that you have been able to think about that. How was it for you to think about it?"

For anxious or split subjects, this type of modulation seems to render the perspective of the approaching session less anxiety-inducing. They understand, in the end, that the therapist takes more responsibility for the dialogue in the beginning and he or she will guide them progressively to a more elaborative working through of the complex experiences that they have been confronted with. It is necessary to frequently verify these clients' emotional states and not let the dialogue develop for too long in a zone where emotion is absent or where they are split, which with these clients often comes down to the same thing. When the tone becomes monotone, the visual contact becomes dull, the answers tend to become banal, it is important to verify the level of emotion and to do so more often. One of the best ways to maintain the client's affect is to use interventions that slow them down or that stop at times of emotion, and to do this the instant that emotion becomes present, even very slightly. The following sequence demonstrates very well the work of the chain of emotions. The client, that we will call Lucien, had participated with me in an experiential group two years ago.

Cl: I would like to do some work with you.

Th: OK, I'm all yours Lucien.

Cl: What? You remember me?

Th: Of course …

Cl: … [emotional]

Th: What's happening?

Cl: I am touched that not only you remember me, my name, but that you called me by my first name straight away. I thought I would have to introduce myself, tell you who I was, what is going on in my life.

Th: I imagine that you are touched in a place where you have already known a lot of pain.

Cl: Yes! My pain is that it seems to me that nobody ever remembers
        me. I was, I think, a sort of one child too many. A forgotten
        child. Sometimes I said to myself that I could have not come
        home from school and nobody would have noticed. I was the
        youngest, always behind compared to the others. I could run
        all I wanted, I never caught up with anyone.

Th: I imagine that this pain that you're telling me, is the sadness,
        the pain of someone for whom something is missing. Some-
        one who has had to grieve for something.

Cl: Yes. That's the way I feel. Like I'm grieving for something.

Th: What are you grieving for?

Cl: I think I had to grieve for my importance, grieving for want-
        ing to count for someone, to be someone unique who exists
        whom one remembers.

Th: Do you remember seeing in the eyes of your father or mother,
        joy or happiness that you were there.

Cl: No I don't think so ....

Th: Do you remember your father's eyes?

Cl: No ...

Th: Do you remember your mother's eyes?

Cl: ... No

Th: Do you know the colour of their eyes?

Cl: ... No ... [At each no he is getting sadder and sadder.]

Th: One could almost imagine you were an orphan. [We can talk
        of the inner or effective orphan.]

Cl: But that's absurd. I wasn't an orphan. They had to be there.
        They created me and they must have noticed me some time.

Th: When you say that, what do you feel?

Cl: I feel afraid. Is it possible that they never looked after me?

Th: And if that was the case?

Cl: [He looks at me in silence. His eyes are big and seem to carry
        an expression of terror. He shakes, trembles.] It's like I'm go-
        ing to die.

Th: Now what is there?

Cl: I feel angry, a rage ... against them. And that makes me very
        afraid ....

Starting from the experience of a surface emotion, an elaboration
in a descending spiral seeks to connect the surface reality with an

experience that was constitutive of identity and joined to the Self by stopping the metabolic process of the developmental issues of attachment.

This type of intervention, in addition to adding to the construction of the meaning of experience, may lead to some elements of restoration being brought together. Often, these subjects have not been held closely enough to sense that they are in the world. They have not sufficiently known the experience of being accompanied and contained in their discoveries of the world and their internal world. To be closely followed and accompanied by a person that is not afraid of being swept away by their terror and their rage contributes to reactivating the developmental process that was interrupted a long time ago.

Restoration and the real relationship

In order to complete the therapeutic work, these clients need to experience an attachment relationship with a figure that is sufficiently stable and sufficiently good. This figure is the therapist. The relationship must permit them to access transitional spaces. The ideal position of the Gestalt therapist is situated, according the theory of Self in the middle zone, at the same time present but detached, active in their vigilance, but sufficiently absent to leave the transitional space to the Other where they can contact these experiential places that the therapist does not always understand, without worrying about it. The therapist and the client can stay there, together, calm. This experience is important for the client who can in this manner succeed in being alone, in peace, and in security.

The following sequence demonstrates this aspect. A client who had been in therapy for two years was waiting in the waiting room. He started reading a poster on the wall: the craftsman's prayer. At the moment when I arrived, he was finishing his reading and was visibly emotional. He entered into my office and, seeing his emotional state, I said to him, "Did the craftsman's prayer touch you?" He answered me by deflecting a little, "Yes. It was very interesting. Where did you get this prayer?" In order not to neutralize his experience I said to him, "You asked me where I got it and I asked you where you put it?" He became emotional again and started talking about his past in a way that he had never done before. I learnt that his mother had wanted him to be a preacher. Then he said, "It is funny, because it is not a religious prayer, but it is a prayer that touched me a lot." At that moment he was not really looking at me but rather behind me where my bookshelf was.

Th: What are you doing?
Cl: I am looking at your books.
Th: I think I disturbed you when I came into the waiting room; I don't think you had finished doing something that was important for you. In fact, it's OK with me if you finish it.
Cl: What do you mean?
Th: I interrupted you; you were in the middle of doing something!

After a brief hesitation he got up and returned to the waiting room in order to finish reading the prayer. When he came back he seemed bigger. He was radiant, showing a real feeling of satisfaction. He went back to looking at my bookshelves.

Th: I think I'm still interrupting!
Cl: No, I want you to be here!
Th: Would you like to look around in my office?
Cl: Oh, yes I would really like that.
Th: Ha, well do it! Do it and I'm going to work at my table, I won't leave. When you are ready to talk to me, ready to be with me, you tell me. Go on, take your time.

He is obviously happy; he is showing the emotion of a child that can look around his dad's papers. He is very touched to be able to do it. For ten minutes he did not cast a glance at me. I no longer existed. Then he looked at me as if he was surprised to see me there.

Th: You look like you've come back from far away.
Cl: Yes! If only you knew where I was .... Now I feel like telling you, but go back to your place.

After I went back to my place, he started telling me everything that he had imagined with the objects in my office. There were statues, a sand timer, African masks, American Indian objects, etc.

Th: Who are we now, you and I?
Cl: You? You are my shaman.

Th: Which is the object that touched you the most?
Cl: It was your peace pipe!
Th: With whom would you like to smoke it?
Cl: I would like to smoke it with my father .... Er ... do you smoke?

This man had passed half an hour in a transitional space, a sort of "middle country" between the real and fantasy, a space where he did not have to look after me. I was not an intrusion and he could unfold in this secure space. He had never before believed that this was possible. He could be with me and yet be alone. He could be peaceful, safe without having to take me into account. Often people that are deprived on the attachment side have not reached this developmental phase. They have had to look after those bigger than themselves or they were not correctly looked after and they have never been able to experience the feeling of security.

In order to heal themselves, they must learn to grieve for all that they want, that they never got, and that they will never have. They are grieving for the attachment and the attention that they needed so much. There is a paradox here because they must in fact grieve for something that they have never known and that may take a long time to find! Somebody must tell them that they will never again be three months old, that that time is past. There is a difficult line of intervention for a therapist. The therapist must cultivate hope and support restoration. However, their clients will never again be three months old and they cannot, at 30 years old, have what they should have had at three months. All the same, they can learn to celebrate what they do have, what there is in their lives now, and what they might have later. But, we must remember, they will never again have the experience that was missing in their past.

The man in the case study wanted to smoke the peace pipe with his father but his father was dead, and what is more he died cursing him! Let us go back to the dialogue:

Cl: Would you find it too much to ask, if in my heart, I think of you as my father?
Th: Would that mean that you want to smoke the peace pipe with me?
Cl: [After a long silence.] No, the peace pipe is smoked after the war, with you I am at peace!

These clients must grow up a bit. The destiny of the "inner child" is not to stay a child but to grow up. To find the inner child consists in going and fetching him and allowing him to grow up. This is what is done in psychotherapy. During the course of this transformation, it is necessary to work within the limits of the client. The therapist himself is called upon to age as a parent. Often he starts with a small baby. Eventually, the baby-client grows up and the therapist ages with him.

In the preceding case, I would never have allowed the client to search among my books from the first day nor even in the first year, for several reasons. Firstly, my books and the objects that decorate my work place represent something for me. When I let somebody touch them, it is significant. For a long time the client was too young to put his nose in those books, to touch those things. It would have appeared intrusive and voyeuristic to me if he had done it, because he could have "broken dad's objects". At the time when I invited him to do it he was old enough to do it.

When the client is a young infant in the regressive sense of the term, the therapist must respond to needs that he senses, because from this space the client does not have the words to ask for them. At this stage the therapist would be wrong to ask the child to recognize its own needs. Sometimes he gets impatient and confronts the client by asking them what they want from the therapist. If the client presents with an attachment problem, they can answer, but the answer will come from the adult and evolved part of themselves. The part of them that really needs something is not capable of answering the question.

In addition, the work on attachment is better served by interventions that are open to uncertainty, to vagueness. A client might say that they no longer know why they are there. The therapist could then answer: "I think that you don't quite know why you are here, but at the same time you are here and I want you to continue to come here. I think that, for the moment, you come here to meet with somebody regularly and that is already a good thing!" The therapist says it for the client because the client is not capable of saying it themselves. When the client starts to babble, to construct their words, to in fact grow up, the therapist begins to respond to the babbled need. If the therapist gets impatient or continues to anticipate the needs of the client because they do not seem capable of expressing it, the therapist is not helping them to grow up. It is much more efficient to tolerate the time that the client takes to construct their words, even approximately, to let them babble, to say more or less, to get it wrong, to go back on themselves, than to speak for them. They are on the brink; it is not the right time to ask for more clarity.

When the client is even bigger, the therapist no longer responds through anticipation of needs, nor those that are babbled. He or she responds to the need that is expressed. A therapist might say: "You seem to have a need, but at the same time, I notice that for today, you are not asking me for anything." One day my client said to me: "I'm not asking for anything because I know that my therapy has reached its end. I know that we are going to finish soon and I'm nostalgic for the times when you seemed to guess what I needed!" Another said, towards the end of his therapy: "I know it is finished, I know that it is time that I left and I know that I'm stretching it out, that I don't want to leave. But I know that I will leave. I would like to do something crazy like I did in the beginning, to arrive in pieces, so that you look at me with tenderness, so that you pick me up and you explain to me what has happened. I feel like those children who need someone to tell them about their childhood. Tell me about the beginning of my therapy. Tell me what it was like when I was little." So I said to him: "Suppose you tell me about it?"

One thing that these clients must learn (and that needs a lot of clarity on the therapist's part) is that a need is not necessarily bad simply because it cannot be satisfied. Those clients missing something in terms of attachment have learnt to no longer have needs because nobody was there to satisfy them. In order to suffer no more, they have learnt to ignore them. They have deduced that their needs are bad and that even their love was bad. That is why it is common to hear them say, "It's too much, I ask too much of those around me, I need too much love." They are looking for a reparative response that we could formulate in the following way: "I don't know if your need is too big, but what I do know is that what you are asking me for, I cannot give you. That doesn't say anything about your demand, it says something about me, about my situation!" When the facts are presented like this the client can start to see, for example that his schizo-affective mother, hospitalized every two or three months, was not capable of reassuring him.

It was not his demand that was bad, it was that she was not capable of responding.

For West and Keller (1994), the fundamental objective of the treatment of attachment pathologies is the following: the client must come to grieve for the experience that he did not fully live and yet that he felt entitled to have. We arrive in this world and from the simple fact we are human, we "know" that we have a right to have a mother who is present and a father who protects us. When we do not have this, we "know" that we are experiencing something that is not normal. That is the reason why West and Keller affirm that these clients must grieve for something they have not known. It is a very particular grieving: that of an experience that they sense was their due, but which they did not have.

To sum up ...

The detection of attachment pathologies first relies on the identification of impasses in contact that resemble an attachment pathology. We notice what in field 3 (current relationships in life today) contains clues to a secure, schizoid-avoidant or anxious-ambivalent organization. We have to ask ourselves about the experience of the client in the seven sets of clinical manifestations of attachment. In field 1, that of the therapeutic relationship, we can note that the client tends to live out with us a schizoid-avoidant or an anxious-ambivalent repetition. As to field 4, the question is the ratio of risk to resilience factors that the client was exposed to in the early stages of his development.

The treatment of attachment pathologies demands, firstly and above all, a good understanding of the archaic character of this issue, often hidden under surface adjustments associated with an intimate and fluid rapport with the attachment issues of the therapist. In taking on this weighty project, the therapist must be prepared to understand the time it will take and the stages that must be passed through. Finally, only those who can accept the role of parent to a client, who can permit him to grow up, and who is willing to age alongside him as a parent, will be able to access their resources and the empathic resonance that will be necessary to accompany the client.

CHAPTER SIX

Self-esteem issues

The concept of self-esteem has captured the attention of a good number of contemporary theoreticians. More often associated with narcissism in the psychoanalytic tradition, self-esteem has also been studied and commented on from a humanistic-existential angle, notably by Nathaniel Branden (1984). Among contemporary psychodynamic authors, the work of McWilliams (1994), Johnson (1987, 1994), Gabbard (1994), as well as Gunderson and Phillips (1998), offers a useful developmental point of view based on Kohut's or Kernberg's ideas. Before addressing the theme of the development of self-esteem, let us explain the parameters of our field of interest. When writing about self-esteem, I shall refer to the developmental issue as it has been studied since the 1970s, by humanistic psychologists, as well as those of the psychodynamic school, such as Kohut. When I use the term narcissism and its derivatives, I shall rather be referring to the pathological indicators of the phenomenon.

The problem of narcissism at the heart of the therapeutic dynamic

The concepts of narcissism and of self-esteem are so often linked in contemporary theory that it is easy to jump to conclusions, one of which is to link wounded self-esteem and narcissistic vulnerability with the pathology of the same name. But all personality structures have a narcissistic function: to protect self-esteem through certain specific defences.

In fact psychological health requires a certain narcissistic sensibility. Narcissism is a fundamental support for being able to defend ourselves in a hostile situation, to affirm our opinions, to offer our contribution, to relate to others. The problem of self-esteem is necessarily interwoven into the therapeutic process by the incontrovertible fact that *all* psychotherapy rests on the dynamics linked to self-esteem or narcissism. Thus work in therapy can only proceed if we recognize implicit flaws in the Self. The therapeutic process therefore rests upon questioning certain methods of defence and adaptation, which hitherto have protected the Self. In the end, a redefining of the very basis of self-esteem is the price we must pay if the therapy is to succeed. Psychotherapy, which is transformational in its essence, presupposes a certain destructuring which, at least provisionally, puts identity in danger. This process is much more complex in the case of clients presenting with a true narcissistic structure. The narcissistic personality is organized around automatic responses in cognition and affect, and behaviours that are enduring and independent of situations and contexts. These elements allow us to distinguish between narcissistic pathology in the personality, and vulnerabilities and normal defences of the same name.

A socio-syntonic pathodynamic

The concept of personality disorder, as we saw earlier, must be treated with care, or else there is a risk of sliding towards a sort of psychosocial eugenics. Do mad societies exist? If the answer is yes, is it mad to be "normal"? When he works with personality-disordered clients, the responsible therapist works at the very core of these questions. So, how do we repair pathological narcissistic suffering in the world? Without slipping into a superficial criticism of society, we may still ask ourselves what it is in the nature of present Western society that sees as normal pathogenic structures that breed anxiety, depression, and indeed actively encourage the active pursuit of what is toxic.

For example, the world of professional sport is often the scene of bidding wars, since victory at any cost is all that matters. Being first overrides all other considerations. Does not the world of high performance sport illustrate a worrying new value for social inclusion: winning at any price?

In the political sphere, the valuing of spin over substance has become commonplace.

Family law today allows just one of the partners in a marriage to decide on divorce, whatever the consequences to the family and the community. Diderot, one of the French Encyclopaedists judged that marriage was indispensable for society and intolerable for the individual. Our society seems to have concluded that individual happiness is more important than commitment to another.

So, unless he lives like a hermit, the average citizen finds himself bombarded with messages proclaiming a hatred of aging, encouraging envy, and commercializing identity. Advertising is well known to use psychological methods that exploit narcissism for commercial gain.

Some clinical manifestations linked to narcissistic issues

What clinical signs can alert the psychotherapist to unfinished developmental issues in the area of self-esteem? Firstly, in the client's life the therapist may notice a predominant preoccupation around the choice of object. The partner must, above all, be *presentable* or better, a source of pride. The partner must also be willing to take the role of an admiring public. Secondly, the greater the client's vulnerability to criticism, the more the clinical situation needs to be seen as presenting unfinished issues of self-esteem. Finally, people in the grip of this issue often suffer from a sort of social isolation that serves the function of protecting a Self that is too fragile to maintain itself in social situations. Such people often find it hard to ask for help, owing to an underlying sense of shame that is easily reactivated when they feel vulnerable.

In the therapeutic relationship, we must be on the look-out for a marked lack of self-responsibility. These people tend to vent their frustrations on those around them. They are "driven to ...", they "end up by ...", yet rarely see their part in these impasses. Their vulnerability to criticism may result in countertransferential responses that interfere with the process of change. One often sees that this extreme vulnerability to criticism leads them to re-experience old injuries that they believe they have sustained in therapy. Often, with a greater or lesser degree of awareness, they set about derailing the therapeutic process in an attempt to induce feelings of guilt or even shame in the therapist. And certainly, they try to establish a climate in which successive cycles of idealization and devaluation will flourish.

A view of the evolution of concepts pertinent to the study of narcissism

There are many views on the developmental and pathological world of narcissism. Let us draw upon some of the classical writers who may be of use to us. (The reader will find references to works that will help him to pursue this interest.)

Freud (1914) and drive theory

Although Freud was not the first to employ the term "narcissism" in psychology, (Havelock Ellis had used it in 1898 to describe perverted behaviour characterized by exclusive self love), it was Freud who first used it in a clinical sense. In 1914, Freud used the term primary narcissism to describe an early, predifferentiated, stage of development in which erotic desire is directed at the Self (p. 76). He used the term "secondary narcissism" to describe the withdrawal from the object and directing the libido towards the Self, in cases of loss or failure, leading at best to a sort of megalomania and at worst to psychotic states such as schizophrenia. This is the first reference to the famous "U model", where the object-seeking libido and the narcissistic libido relate conflictually. The more one empties, the more the other fills up. This libidinal investment of the ego is characteristic of psychotic states. The ego ideal appears, later, as an image of self that embodies our highest aspirations: a crucial basis for self-esteem.

Freud later (1931) described the narcissistic personality as having no tension between ego and super-ego. There is no great preponderance of erotic needs, and the principal interest is in self-preservation. The ego carries a great deal of aggression, which shows in a propensity for displacement activity.

Reich and defensive grandiosity

For Reich (1926), healthy narcissism is the regulator of self-esteem. The phallic-narcissistic character differs from the compulsive and the hysteric. Whereas the compulsive is mainly inhibited, automatic, and depressive, and the hysteric nervous, apprehensive, and labile, the phallic-narcissistic character is typically self-assured, arrogant, expansive, vigorous, and often impressionable. The more neurotic the interior mechanism, the worse adapted the behaviour. As for the body type, narcissists seem often to belong to Kretschmer's (1931) "sporty types". Facial expression is usually hard, with masculine characteristics accentuated. These people are generally aloof, cold, and reserved. In love relationships, the narcissistic libido is valued above the object-seeking libido and a mixture of more or less well-disguised sadistic traits may be observed. Pathological narcissism is the defensive elaboration of grandiosity in response to poor self-esteem.

Fairbairn (1954) and the object model

According to Fairbairn (1954), the narcissistic child withdraws into the Self and does not seek real contact. At first, each child seeks for contact outside itself. This is not a sexual or libidinal drive, as Freud believed, but a response to a fundamental need for relationship, an energy essential for life and survival. However, if the child does not have access to a suitable available person, he directs his energies inwards. This may be the case with hospitalized children or for those whose mothers are not emotionally responsive.

Fairbairn breaks with Freud's determinist model. According to him, there is a need and a trauma. There is no drive but there is a choice. The frustrated child seeks a transitional object, whether it be his thumb or something else. Some children give up their quest for an object in order to survive in a rejecting or over-frustrating environment. These children withdraw into their own inner fortress. The primary task for the therapist is to meet the child and thence to lead him forth to form relationships with external objects. Here, what appears as attachment to the Self, is actually a compensatory attachment to internal objects.

Kohut and the bipolar self (1966, 1971)

Kohut places normal and pathological narcissism on a sort of continuum. Narcissistic needs for self-affirmation and for soothing are life-long. The only change is in the way we get these needs met. From this developmental perspective, idealization becomes a necessary process for consolidating the Self. The idealized parent carries the projected perfection and happiness of the primary and normal narcissistic states. Idealizing relationships are progressively introjected and give meaning and direction for our aspirations.

Having redefined narcissism in this way, Kohut sets out to identify and describe the trajectory of healthy narcissism in normal development. Throughout development, the individual needs significant others, called *selfobjects*, whose essential function is to support the Self in different phases of development, such as the expression of ambitions and talents and the construction of a personal ethic.

Kernberg and narcissistic perversion

Kernberg created his theory of narcissism from a clinical sample of inpatients and outpatients. Most of his subjects presented a picture of primitive affect, aggression, and arrogance, with an aura of haughty grandiosity, which coexisted alongside a degree of timidity.

In his view, the narcissistic structure rests upon the primitive defences and object relations that are typical in low-functioning personalities. This structure results from the fusion of the ideal Self, the ideal object and the grandiose Self. Grandiose representations of the Self are viewed as a defence against object-dependence. The function of idealization is to defend the Self against rage, envy, mistrust, and devaluation. Kernberg believes that narcissistic personalities belong in the low-functioning group. Even though the majority have a more cohesive and better functioning ego than low-functioning patients, some present with an obviously limited ability to function.

Miller and the gifted child

The gifted and cherished child often becomes a narcissistic adult. This gift of nature may become a curse. Miller (1991) demonstrates the means by which some people cannot draw nourishment from their own achievements which, in their eyes, are never good enough. Miller believes strongly that some children, sensing the emotional insecurity of their parents, attempt to soothe through displaying their gifts and talents. Thus they gain their parents' love, but in doing so lose the attention to their own needs that they so deeply crave.

In adulthood, these children often choose the helping professions. They know how to read the signals of another's unconscious needs. Unfortunately, they also unconsciously refuse to satisfy their own needs and thus cannot develop to become the persons they might be. This makes them prone to depression or to a grandiosity whose function is to exorcise their latent depression.

Normal development of self-esteem

If we adopt a more Kohutian view that suggests that the development of the Self by-passes the consolidation of self-esteem, what indications do we have that the task has been reasonably completed?

In addition to good self-esteem, a confidant and empathic disposition towards the Other is discernable, yet matched by a capacity to defend against the possibility of attack by the Other. Such people cultivate ideals that are well assimilated and reflected upon, and that give meaning to their experience and direction to their life. They have enough creative aggression to pursue their ideals. In short, their motto could be: *I am by nature imperfect, limited, and worthy. So is the Other.*

Developmental failure particular to narcissism

People with either interrupted or perverted narcissistic development tend to have poor self-esteem. Faced with the Other, they are mistrustful and unempathic. Faced with aggression from the Other, they may neither be able to defend themselves, nor to take steps to understand the attack and how to defend against or respond to it.

Their ideals tend to be grandiose and introjected rather than assimilated. The ideal is a central dimension of their pathology in the sense that their effort towards attaining their ideal isolates them and their inability to attain it brings on depression. This impasse is at the heart of innumerable depressions. The impasse takes the form of an aggressively expressed frustration about how what they do is never good enough contrasted with a similarly expressed aggression directed towards the environment that failed them in their pursuit of the ideal.

The central tenet of their motto, in contrast with the previous one, might be expressed thus: *My true Self is indispensable to the existence of the relationship yet my true Self is intolerable to the Other and to myself.*

Pathogenesis and dilemmas that are specific to self-esteem

Let us now address the question of development that is specific to self-esteem, and above all, that of the obstacles to this development. The authors referred to above have each in their own way both risk factors and resilience factors. I shall look in turn at all the elements that constitute the developmental field and, supported by clinical research and contemporary writers, I shall set out certain factors that tend to appear in the developmental history of clients presenting with damage to their self-esteem.

The organism

What is there to say about the innate aspect of the pathologies of self-esteem? Not much. The bipartite model of personality presents a logical relationship between two universes: temperament and character. However, the organic dimension of character is hard to quantify. Some writers have been able to put forward plausible, albeit anecdotal, hypotheses based on clinical observation. Thus Kernberg, for example, believes that grandiose narcissists are constitutionally more aggressive than most people. In addition, he believes they have poor tolerance for the anxiety that accompanies their aggressive drives, resulting in a relative inability to admit or recognize either their aggression or their envy. From another perspective, we can add Miller's idea that this group contains individuals who are more sensitive than most to non-verbal communication. These "gifted" children will be more sensitive to narcissistic exploitation.

Their natural intuitive talents may be exploited by a narcissistically fragile parent or parents.

We may consider the hypothesis of a factor of organic risk, or a temperament made up of a mixture of aggression and heightened anxiety and accompanied by a powerful non-verbal sensitivity.

The environment

A common factor seems to emerge from the childhood memories of these clients: within the family, they were always subject to evaluation, as was everything else. This car was better than that one, this uncle was more generous than the other one, this writer was useless, the neighbours were always trying to keep up with the Joneses. As for the child, everything he did was subject to comparison. He should be doing better than so-and-so at school, play the lead in the school play, know his alphabet before he was two, and his tables pretty soon after that!

This atmosphere of constant comparison is pernicious, because it becomes "normal" for the child. He comes to believe that he can only be enough or satisfactory if he gets a prize. Being constantly in the spotlight leads the vulnerable child to develop an internal landscape where the essential (and often stimulating) necessity to do well is in constant opposition to the anxiety of never doing well-enough.

It appears that these unfinished issues are transmitted over generations. And unfinished issues in one parent or, more to the point, in both, are an important risk factor. With regard to this, McWilliams (1994) suggests that one can gain insight into the narcissistic disposition of the parent if one asks them about the expected baby. The more the parent seems to know what the baby will be like, the more his or her welcoming the new baby into the world will be narcissistically charged The baby will be born into a project that was fixed before he was born. There is a major risk that the child will become what the parent has imagined and wished for. If this prediction comes true, it is often at the cost of the child's separation and individuation.

Meeting

What happens when the vulnerable organism meets an unfavourable environment? Most parents are disposed to look at their child from an amalgam of narcissistic needs and true empathy. It is natural for parents to wish their child to have things they did not have. This encourages the child and, let us add, society and the species to aspire to higher things. This is what Kohut calls the natural and developmental function of ambition.

Moreover no one, not even A. S. Neil and his followers at Summerhill, has ever educated a child without criticising. The corrective necessity of adequate criticism, linked to the child's developmental stage, embodies the function of ideals in the Kohutian sense. Each child up to a certain point is treated as the narcissistic extension of its parents. When this aspiration and these ideals are presented and lived with empathy and moderation, the child loves to be its parents' pride and joy.

The early relational environment is particularly indispensable to the development of narcissism: it embodies the ideal. The parents must be psychologically capable of welcoming infantile grandiosity, as long as necessary. But some parents cannot tolerate this natural phase of childish all-powerfulness and seek to shatter the illusion, to "break" the character and the spirit of the child. Miller challenges this in her work. Other kinds of parents identify with rather than empathically appreciate the idealization and, when the time comes, cannot allow the child gradually to recognize their limitations and progressively separate from them in order to turn to other objects of idealization and sources of inspiration. Some parents cannot bear their child to have any self-doubt. They do not admit his failures and seek to restore the illusion of all-powerfulness rather than helping the child to accept his limitations and still retain his self-esteem.

A second task or function of the early relational environment is to focus and contain ambition, aggression, and anxiety. In the development of his self-esteem, the child needs to follow his own ambition without shaping himself to fit a parent's ambition. He must also learn to mobilize aggression appropriately for the pursuit of his ideals and the satisfaction of his ambitions. So, the parent should be capable of gauging the quality of this aggression and allow him room to concentrate and complete an adequate and useful action. If the parent himself is too vulnerable, he may, as Miller tells us, fail as the guardian of his child's ambition and aggression and act in such a way as to nip these in the bud. Indeed, he may see in his child the expression of his own aggression that has been long repressed. This runs the risk of communicating complacency about the child's true strength and the child is at risk of having this strength perverted into an unbounded and unfocused rage that has no clear objective.

Therefore, the most fundamental object of the meeting between the Self and its environment is, without doubt, this ongoing experiential dialogue at the heart of which must be reflected the child's experience and developmental progress. One useful lesson that Kohut teaches the therapist is to take on the incomplete parental task of being with the client while making sense of the client's developmental experiences. Adequate reflection of developmental experience does not mean applauding everything and giving even the most ordinary performance a standing ovation! It is surely the case that, as a result of normal neurological maturation, the child feels in his body and in his mind that not everything he does is perfect, that he is not always the best, and that sometimes he will get things wrong. The person who is denied the experience of setbacks and difficulties does not get on any better than the one who has the opposite experience. Indeed, adequate reflection of developmental experience is firstly to allow it. It is holding up a mirror which is neither distorting nor indulgent, but kindly. It avoids muddling up love, pride, and admiration.

Finally, and in order to avoid the pitfalls described by Miller, the parent should take care to reality-test the child's intuitive sensibility. When the child has a feeling about something, when he looks to the adult to help him in testing reality, he must be met by someone who can and will honour this young mind, this burgeoning sensibility. A parent most often contributes to the degradation of healthy narcissism, and its mutation into perverted narcissism, by denying and distorting reality. The best parent at the self-esteem stage of development knows how to respond to the child's sensitivity, but also knows where to draw the line between how much reality the child can take and what is too much for him.

The human environment becomes unhealthy and unassimilable when it refuses to cope with idealization or is not suited to be the ideal in the child's eyes. Also, according to how he responds to anxiety, the parent may produce, over time, a relationship that gets in the way of self-esteem. Anyone who denigrates, denies, or disbelieves his child's anxiety contributes to setting up an inevitable split, as a result of which, in later life, anxiety will be projected, indeed induced in the Other.

So, when the parent, instead of adequately reflecting the developmental experiences of the child, distorts them by reflecting them in accordance with his own narcissistic issues, he contributes to an experience of loss of Self, which heralds an internal void, one of the most prominent clinical characteristics of pathological narcissism.

What is the result of these introjects and internalizations? The vulnerable child who grows up in a high-risk family certainly feels himself very important and very validated, but only in the role he is called upon to play. He feels that if anyone discovers his other functions and affects, particularly selfishness, hostility, and anxiety, he will be rejected and humiliated. This encourages what Winnicott calls the False Self, presenting to the world what one has learnt is acceptable.

From this follows an interruption of the natural process of narcissistic maturation. The experience of grandiosity and envy has been unchecked and these issues remain unfinished. The child and later the adult remains blocked. He may get stuck in idealizing the Other, in infantile grandiosity, or in anxiety. Ambition and aggression are either inhibited, or accentuated in the flight from anxiety. He cannot use his intuitive sensitivity to make contact. He copes with this unfinished issue—his unchecked envy and grandiosity—by holding it back and at the same time protecting the suffering part of these repressed or split-off experiences by setting up (in conscious experience) idealization and devaluation of Self and other.

If we can accept these few etiological hypotheses, let us now consider the clinical phenomenon of the narcissistic impasse in adulthood: DSM's diagnostic criteria remind us how unconscious reproduction of developmental dilemmas are manifested phenomenologically. Thus, lack of empathy and exaggerated sensitivity to other people's opinions result in the narcissist doing to the Other what was done to him. He exploits the Other in interpersonal relationships. He has been important to his parents, not for who he was but for what he represented. Therefore, the Other must be useful in some way. He becomes the extension of this perfect Other, be he lover, mentor, therapist, or any hero figure: "If I am like X, I can't go wrong." These people grow up in solitude, expecting and seeking a demi-god. This expectation seems to be worth more than the presence of a real person. When the demi-god is finally found, he must stay perfect or else be knocked off his pedestal.

The person who presents with a developmentally narcissistic pathology takes on grandiose objectives to compensate for what feels to him to be a tragic and unforgivable flaw within the Self. He does it at work, in love, in his leisure pursuits, and ... in therapy. Attaining an objective confirms the grandiosity and maintains the narcissistic defence against emptiness and shame. On the other hand, failure activates the experience of narcissistic depression. It reproduces and confirms the tragic flaw and perpetuates the cycle.

To sum up ...

Pathologies of self-esteem and narcissism are the result of a vulnerable organism (constitutionally more aggressive, with poor tolerance of anxiety about its aggressive drives, more sensitive than most to non-verbal communication), meeting an unfavourable developmental environment: whether that be an atmosphere of permanent evaluation, or of narcissistic issues incomplete in one or both parents.

This meeting leads to an interruption or a perversion of a healthy narcissism and the pathogenic relational field is introjected. The energy contained in the narcissistic issue continues to play out in the daily life of the person, without his realizing it. It is acted out through the process of reproduction of the pathogenic field. The reproduction of narcissistic impasses is the result of an unconscious effort to make sense of the person's internal experience.

CHAPTER SEVEN

Treating self-esteem issues

W e shall address the treatment of self-esteem issues from the multiple viewpoints of relational psychotherapy.
The difficulties in making contact that lie at the heart of these pathologies will be understood and worked through from two points of view. These perspectives, adopted and practised in the pluralist vein of contemporary psychoanalysis, are those of Kohut and Kernberg. Historically, they have been involved in rather a conflictual relationship, of which it may be said, if one is not constrained by institutional loyalty, that it says as much if not more about politico-institutional as about clinical disagreement. From Kohut's point of view, narcissistic pathology is the result of arrested development. We imagine that the person who manifests this pathology has been hindered in his normal need to idealize and de-idealize. This point of view is very near to our thinking about the evolution of personality disorders. In reality, personality disorder results from the mixture of risk and resilience factors, in both the biological and the social spheres. When risk factors are greater than resilience factors, the process of development is interrupted or perverted. We begin, in fact, with the two perspectives already described earlier: Kohut's

which considers failure as arrested development and Kernberg's who sees it as a perversion of this process.

By way of comparison, one could say that, according to Kohut, the person who suffers from a pathology of self-esteem is like a plant deprived of water and light. The treatment is obvious: within a psychotherapeutic environment, give him water and light and the person will be in a state to reactivate his development. In real terms, this means that the therapeutic relationship must be willing to accept positive and negative transference. The therapist must work from an empathic position. Easier said than done! Most of us prefer one of the aspects of the positive/negative transference process. Some therapists work with people who need this type of attention but they fail fully to grasp the issue. Thus they feel they are engaged in a therapeutic process that sometimes goes well, sometimes not. It goes well when the main aspect is the positive transference and badly when negative transference is at the forefront. Ideally, we should try to maintain a situation in which both are equally welcome. Affect attunement and empathy, positive and negative transference are seen as two sides of the same phenomenon, both equally necessary.

Those therapists who choose to work without considering the transference, do so in such a way that only one aspect can be worked on, which has the end result that neither really gets addressed. From a relational therapy viewpoint, the therapist must be skilful enough to allow the development of a particular type of transference in order to activate and work on developmental issues. If he is very obviously mainly kind or mainly confronting, the client may have difficulty setting up the sort of relationship that he needs. The therapeutic position is like giving the client a second shot at development. For this to happen, the therapist adjusts his presence and his participation in the dialogue in order to re-create the relational conditions that existed for the client when the process was halted or derailed. Eventually he and the client will get to the place where the developmental issue is lying fallow.

When the therapist has succeeded in turning back the psychological clock to the point of the unfinished developmental phase, he and the client can pick up and re-knit the developmental threads. This is why this type of psychotherapy makes the relationship the basis for the developmental space. The therapist who works with self-esteem issues in Kohut's way offers himself as a parental figure, or *selfobject*. This differs from other psychoanalytic traditions where the transference unfolds in the face of the therapist's welcoming neutrality. In the Kohutian tradition, the therapist knows from the outset that he will be called upon to be a parent and to accompany the client in the developmental process. Because of this, he is not forced to hold back. He is active, benevolent, empathic, "containing".

Kernberg's point of view is radically different. He does not see narcissistic pathology as a problem of arrested development. He sees it as more of a structural problem, resulting from early deregulation, so that the client has retreated behind primitive defences that are qualitatively different from normal functioning. Kernberg proposes that narcissists do things that others do not. The contrast with Kohut is clear: for him, narcissists do *badly* or *too much* the things that others do *less* or *well*. Kernberg believes that narcissists develop styles of object relating that are different from those of healthy people.

If we take up the plant analogy, Kernberg does not believe in a plant that lacked water and light, but rather in a plant that has mutated, has hybridized, and grown all wrong. It is different from what nature intended, as if a maple branch was growing from a lilac tree! If we allow this point of view, we accept that giving water and light will encourage the growth of the hybrid part. For Kernberg, treatment of self-esteem issues, when they are pathologically narcissistic, is therefore radically different.

This form of treatment is like pruning the aberrant parts of the plant. In plain terms, it is confronting grandiosity, in the Self and in the other, while interpreting these as defences against shame. Grandiosity is the aberration that Kernberg discerns in the narcissistic personality. It is not a developmental stage any more than envy is. Strictly speaking, we could imagine that at no point does Kernberg see envy or shame as natural processes.

There is a great difference between Kohut's and Kernberg's theories …. At first glance we may imagine that Kohut's treatment is gentle, warm, and welcoming and Kernberg's much more confrontational. Actually, seen on video, Kernberg reveals himself to be a remarkably gentle, sensitive, and empathic therapist. His theories are different from his practice. There is still work to be done in the dissemination of his ideas in order for the clinician to grasp a more elegant clinical use of the techniques of pruning and confronting. Kernberg's technique sheds light on what is aberrant in the client's experience. What Kernberg reflects back to the client is not "When you do that you are being nasty to me ...", but "When you do that you show me your pain ...." His empathic resonance is clear in this type of intervention.

The controversy between these two authors, these two systems, and these two American psychoanalytical traditions continues. One could say that it happened through the fates intervening, for Kohut died in 1981. Kernberg is very much alive and very active. Even today, in Kernberg's view, Kohut proposed a supportive psychotherapy. Those who know the psychoanalytic milieu and culture will understand that this is tantamount to an insult. Supportive psychotherapy is little more than counselling! This supportive psychotherapy would be suitable for especially disorganized (close to low-functioning) or psychotic narcissistic clients. However, Kohut's students and the post-Kohutians assert that Kohut developed his model from working with patients on the couch, in the context of classical psychoanalysis appropriate for his style and his inclination. The narcissistic personalities that Kohut refers to are those with whom he was working three or four times a week, and whom he only put on the couch after many face-to-face sessions. We might deduce that these clients had a reasonably high level of functioning, or else he would not have let them use the couch. On the other hand, some Kohutians support the assertion that Kernberg's approach ought to suit more damaged patients.

Today, many people wonder if in the final analysis we are talking about two categories of quite different clients. One contemporary writer, Arthur Modell (1986), has attempted to understand the debate between Kohut and Kernberg. He concluded that Kernberg's model is better indicated for damaged clients. Today, Modell and several others believe that Kohut and Kernberg were both right, but that they were not talking about the same people. They did not have the same practice and did not choose clients in the same way. Kohut's treatment plan was designed and suitable for the patients he had. From the Kohutian point of view, the patients of whom Kernberg speaks are low-functioning patients. And their narcissism is indeed more aberrant and more akin to the idea of the *hybrid* than to arrested development.

One can see the risk of having a Kernbergian type of client and working with him in a Kohutian way. One would be in danger of driving the roots of the narcissistic aberration even deeper, helping it to flourish. At the end of the day, one would end up with an even more "toxic" narcissist. On the other hand, if one works like Kernberg with someone with arrested development, one risks his undergoing exactly the same experience as that which interrupted his development, in other words, an unempathic stance and a rejection of his expressivity. In the final analysis, one cannot, without another way of judging them, deny the ideas of either of these two theoreticians and clinicians who have made their idiosyncratic mark on the history of psychoanalysis and psychotherapy.

So let us consider both points of view and see if we can integrate them into a responsible methodology. Firstly, there is the question: of the two errors that we have mentioned above, which is the less damaging and the more reparable? Working empathically with a perverted narcissist is less damaging than confronting someone whose narcissism has undergone a developmental arrest. And, according to Modell, with clients presenting with problems of self-esteem or narcissism, we should begin by employing congruent empathy, and being attentive and reserved. This approach should be maintained until one feels one has touched on *something* aberrant and perverse. Within a solid relationship, and with enough empathic resonance, there may be moments of confrontation. This is supported by the empathic relationship. Of course, this demands a lot from the therapist, who needs to be vigilant, receptive, and skilled.

Below is a clinical vignette to illustrate our thoughts. Caroline is an elegant young woman, a pharmacist by profession. She has been in therapy for five months at the time of the vignette. In session 22, the previous week, she talked for a long time about her relationship with Peter, with whom she has been going out for 18 months. She found fault with his lack of communication, his lack of feeling, as well as his lack of ambition.

She described a scene where she invited Peter to a "romantic" dinner, in order to get close to him. The conversation at the romantic dinner soon came round to Peter's shortcomings. He left, slamming the door, and called her the next day saying he had been hurt by the turn of events and the relationship.

During this session, the therapist among other things questioned Caroline's process, contrasting the original intention behind the (romantic) dinner and the way it ended.

Th1:   ...

Cl1:   I haven't had a good week. Last week, I left feeling a bit
         wobbly, feeling I hadn't been understood.

Th2:   ...

Cl2:   Afterwards I was upset that I talked to you about Peter the
         way I did. I really got the idea that you saw me as quite a
         fickle girl, whereas I was quite proud of myself. I thought
         I'd finally got to be respected in a relationship. I was really
         surprised at your reaction.

Th3:   What do you mean by "my reaction"?

Cl3:   Well, when you said that Peter was in a trap, for example,
         I thought you were pushing me quite hard ...

Th4:   Hmm. Can you remember what you hoped my reaction
         would be?

Cl4:   I don't know. Perhaps that you find that I'm improving.
         It seemed that if that had happened before, I would have put
         up with it and just left it. Whereas that time I thought I held
         my ground.

Th5:   What's it like for you telling me this now?

Cl5:   It's alright. I am telling it like it is.

Th6:   And how do you think it is for me to hear that?

Cl6:   Well, you seem a bit puzzled. As if I was completely on the
         wrong track.

Th7:   Again, you aren't received as you hoped?

Cl7:   No, it's not that. Last week I felt you were on Peter's side.
         Now it's more like you don't understand what I'm talking
         about ...

Th8:   We're having difficulty meeting, eh? I can't see myself.
         I don't know how I look but really, I don't feel puzzled but
         interested, trying to understand. Obviously you are talking
         to me about something important and which hurts you.

Cl8:   That touches me, you saying that. You see, last week I didn't
         feel that you realized that I was hurting ... What's happen-
         ing? Is it you or me who's inventing things? Is it you or me
         who's off the wall?

Th9:   Lots of questions, eh? On top of the ones that are unan-
         swered from last week ...

Cl9:   Do you think I ask too many questions?

Th10:   I notice how quickly you think I'm criticising you this week. ... In one way, I'm touched by your sensitivity. And in another, I feel I have to be careful. As if I could easily hurt you without meaning to.

Cl10:   You at least would not mean to.

Th11:   What do you mean?

Cl11:   ...

Th12:   You seem sad now ...

Cl12:   [Cries] ... God how difficult it is to be understood. It's not that. It's not you. I mean ... I don't know what I mean.

Th13:   You've got lots to say. Suppose you try to sort it out?

Cl13:   ...

Th14:   One might say that today things are in a muddle and that you are remembering three relationships that are to do with this discomfort, this feeling of misunderstanding. On one hand there's us and what happened last week. You're also remembering your relationship with Peter. And just then you seemed to be talking to me about an old relationship, with your parents perhaps, when you said that if I hurt you it would be by mistake ...

Cl14:   Oh yes. Caroline, the eternal misunderstood ...!

Th15:   Do you see yourself like that ?

Cl15:   It's often like that.

Th16:   ... When you say it like that, at first, it doesn't seem serious. If I got into your way of starting off, I might underestimate the importance of what was happening for you ...

Cl16:   Huh. Worse. Then I could complain of being misunderstood.

Th17:   ...

Cl17:   Still, I'm not going to put up with a bloke who doesn't see me. Would you accept a bloke who doesn't want to grow, stuck in his job, limited?

Th18:   ...

Cl18:   More questions, eh?

Th19:   It's not so much the questions that annoy me. It's rather that by criticising Peter and trying to get me to join in, you seem to be getting away from something that touched you a minute ago.

Cl19:   Oh great. Here we go again. I understand why you're protecting him.

Th20:   We're fighting again. I'm beginning to understand the price of not agreeing with you.

Cl20:   ...

Th21:   If I think about what's happening, it seems that I've only two choices. Do what you want, in which case I'm a good person. Do what I want, in which case I'm devalued. I'm not as good ...

Cl21:   ...

Th22:   What's happening now?

Cl22:   I'm in a muddle. I'm afraid you're angry with me, even though I can see you don't look angry.

Th23:   The difference seems painful ... painful and risky.

Cl23:   [Cries.]

Th24:   Maybe what I was experiencing just now, give in to be appreciated or don't give in and be devalued, is something you know about ...? Perhaps for a long time?

Cl25:   My father and mother were good people. People who worked all their lives to do the best for us. I wouldn't have wanted to disappoint or hurt them.

Th26:   That can't always have been easy ....

Cl26:   ...

Th27:   What did you have to be not to disappoint them or hurt them?

Cl27:   It wasn't that they asked for anything in particular. It's just that they were so proud of us ...

Th28:   Of you ...?

Cl28:   My sister and me. Martine was more of a rebel, headstrong. I've always been closer to them ...

Th29:   Them ...?

Cl29:   To my dad mostly. He took me to my riding lessons .... When I qualified for the jumping team, it was the best present I could have given him. He was so proud .... In the clubhouse, you should have seen him. It was as if he'd been the one who did the jumping. His friends congratulated him, told him how proud he should be of me.

Th30:   And you?

Cl30:   What?

Th31:   ...

Cl31:   I was in seventh heaven. Seeing him so proud after all the sacrifices he'd made.

Th32:   I'm struck by how important it is for you, this pride.

Cl32:   It really was a great moment in my life ...

Th33:   I'm wondering if that's what last week's disappointment was about. You came feeling you'd achieved something and you expected me to recognize you, to be proud of you in a way.

Cl33:   That's true .... And instead you highlighted my mistakes.

Th34:   Like someone you couldn't satisfy?

Cl34:   ...

Th35:   I'm asking myself. It seems you are talking of your parents in two different ways. On the one hand, you describe them as good people that you didn't want to disappoint. On the other, I was in suspense when you mentioned being hurt by mistake.

Cl35:   ...

Th36:   ...

Cl36:   You could say that my mother was the opposite. As if she was afraid I'd get big headed. She always highlighted my mistakes.

Th37:   One might say that this scenario from the past follows you around. Even here with me. As if you haven't been able to finish something important.

Cl37:   But how is it that I'm always doing this? Can I ever finish this quest, this begging for recognition?

Th38:   I hope so.

Cl38:   ... It seems as if no one's ever talked to me like this .... It's funny what's happening. I can see that I could feel hurt by what you say and at the same time it would be dishonest of me ... I know that basically what you say is fair and you say it in a fair way. But you see, I know how to turn on the tears to make you feel bad and take it all back. It's a fruitless game, but you could say that often it's stronger than me. I can see myself slipping into it and I don't know how to do anything else.

Th39:   It seems that this is the first time you've been able to speak about this from such a distance. What's it like to do that?

Cl39:   ... God I'd love to hang on to this moment. I feel right. [Becomes emotional.] And now, I'm thinking about Peter again and I feel I've been unfair to him.

Th40:   Now, does he seem less ... limited to you?

Cl40:   It's frightening to say that about someone. Someone you love ...

Th41:   Sometimes we do funny things to those we love.

Will this young woman react better to empathy or to confrontation? In a way she reacts well to an empathic response and that seems to produce the desired effect. Still, after a while it is time to ask oneself a few questions. The conversation takes the following turn:

Th: I am touched by your sensitivity.

Cl: I'm very glad you said that because last week you didn't say that to me.

She gives the impression of being able to use the therapist's empathy as a means to wear him down, which is not a good sign. If this tendency were to persist, the therapist would have to modify his approach. However, if after a bit of persistence, the therapist's empathic response ends up having the expected response, he can carry on with this type of response.

Having said that, Kohut's view is that there are times when confrontation can also be an empathic response. For instance, a child attacks me and I tell him I love him. My response is not empathic if it does not resonate with the child's affect at this moment. When we are attacked, our instinctive and organic response is not love! A really empathic response also acknowledges the aggression. It is true in development and it is true in therapy.

Even if, in a way, Kernberg can admit that there are developmental hazards in narcissistic pathogenesis, his clinical position is as follows: our work with these clients is not simply a question of setting in motion a relational journey where inappropriate response can be corrected by empathic reflection. The adult narcissist is problematically perverse. Kernberg defines perversity as being the use of love in the service of hate. In other words, the narcissistic client uses the love and empathy of the Other to attack him. This is what Caroline could have done if she had continued to get harder and reproaching the therapist each time he showed empathic consideration for her experience.

This is not a process that can be corrected by simply "reparenting". The narcissistic response is now lodged at the heart of the client's identity. In other words, we cannot receive or treat it as a parent would, but as a "surgeon" would! In the case of an adult client, we cannot hope to reactivate the developmental process before removing the abscess.

Possibilities for exploitation from the perspectives of Kohut and Kernberg within the framework of relational psychotherapy

The cycle of reproduction, recognition, reparation

Narcissistic issues, like all unfinished developmental issues, tend to be repeated in a more or less conscious attempt to complete or maintain them. Thus, the client will repeat narcissistic impasses (constant criticism, idealization, devaluing) in significant contexts in his life. Narcissistic impasses tend particularly to be repeated in three types of significant relationships: the couple relationship, the authority relationship, and the parent-child relationship. So, we need to be prepared to repair narcissistic impasses in clients' relationships with their children, with authority figures, and with their life partners.

Because of the intimacy that develops in the therapeutic relationship it is very likely to reactivate these developmental issues. From one perspective, the therapist, because he manages the context and is presumed to have and may even display specialist knowledge, appears to the client as an authority figure. When the client enters the therapist's consulting room, he generally says to himself, "I'm at his place, he has let me in and he is in charge." Sometimes, the client seems to act as if he is at *his* place and it is up to him to run the show. Mostly, he acts like a junior employee: he does not *really* think he's the boss.

Because the therapist is there on a regular basis, face-to-face, alone with the client, the latter constructs several fantasies of intimacy, sometimes even an erotic transference. The love relationship is the only other relationship where one is alone, often vulnerable, and expected to be open with another. The fantasy of intimacy is bound to arise sooner or later in the therapeutic relationship.

Finally, because the therapist takes on the task of remaking the developmental path, because he cares, inspires, frustrates, he is also a parental figure. One can see that the therapist, by virtue of who he is and without making any particular effort, is in a position to foster the emergence of the three types of relationship—couple, authority, parental—that are likely to activate developmental issues. Mere contact with the therapist is enough for them to be repeated. He should not prevent it happening. On the contrary, he should welcome the client not from a position of benevolent neutrality, nor by holding back from contact (as in the psychoanalytic tradition), but from what Gestaltists call *creative indifference*. The therapist does not yet know where the client needs to meet him and he allows himself to be impregnated by the affective microclimate that the client brings with him. He lets himself have a "taste" and, little by little, he differentiates. The therapist has a sense of what is happening and he does not put up barriers against the client's microclimate.

In order not to damage the process of repetition, he must stop himself from being over-encouraging or too welcoming. He is simply open to the space where repetition occurs. In this initial attitude, there is both welcome and reserve. The reserve allows the client to organize the psychic space between himself and the therapist so that it makes sense to him. All therapists have their vulnerabilities, but all of us must try to contain our desire to appear perfectly good or amazingly perceptive.

One of the things that one can notice in the case of people with difficulties in the area of self-esteem is that on the surface of the dialogue a particular defence blossoms: perfectionism. In these clients perfectionism is a defence against shame: "If I am perfect, I will never have to feel ashamed." The second defence against shame is contempt. In the therapeutic context, the process of repetition has three properties: perfectionism, contempt, and shame. In those with narcissistic issues, the consequence of perfectionism consists in incessant criticism of the Self or the therapist. Caroline is a good example of this style of reproduction. She sets it up with Peter as well as with the therapist and it can also be discerned in field 4 (there and then).

As the therapeutic relationship develops and deepens, a powerful transference in direct proportion to the importance of the narcissistic issue can be seen: an idealization/devaluation transference, two sides of the same phenomenon. However the client does not recognize it as transference. His experience of the therapist is objective and based on fact! In his eyes there is no element of transference in this idealization. He idealizes the therapist because, objectively, he is the best. On the other hand, he may equally devalue the therapist because, objectively, he is mediocre. When trying to work with these reproductions, one must first transform these reactions into an ego dystonic affect. The client must be able to get some distance from and can question what has up to now felt second nature, like a part of him. However, the client is totally immersed in his experience, which does not help him either to stand back or to be receptive to an intervention. One must surface a number of thematic similarities before making an intervention. When one has enough material to say, for example: "It seems that what's happening here and now is like something that happens at other times in other places," this gives a certain distance. The client has to go into that "other time and place" in order to see the resemblance between the two phenomena. If one can establish two, three, or four examples of such thematic similarities, one can create a distance, the first step to an intervention.

So, to Caroline one might say: "I notice that what's happening between us is like what happens with you and Peter and is not unlike what happened between your mother and you." Then one stays there. The next phase begins when the client starts to recognize the thematic affinity or to say something that helps the process of making sense of it all. Then one can begin to give a name to the theme. For example: "Just now you seem to be in such and such a role [judge, for instance] and I am in such and such a role [the accused]." Alternatively: "You might say that in these three situations, someone is persecuting someone else." If that makes sense to her, one might add: "Right now you are acting as if you have to persecute me in order to get me to understand what you are telling me!" Each piece of this sense-making has to be done by both people, within the container of a hermeneutic dialogue. It is not about cutting up an interpretation into three or four successive fragments, but constructing with the client the meaning of his experience.

On the matter of content, this brings to mind Kernberg's process of interpretation: repair then identification of a current object relation with its affective tone. Here always, one must watch for inversion in representations. For example: "You could say now that our roles are reversed! It seems that from your point of view I'm persecuting you!"

This is how Kernberg confronts: "Look what you are doing and see how complex it is, how we are exchanging roles."

A bit later one can see that the client begins to ask himself: "What does this theme mean? What am I trying to achieve by doing things this way?"

Thus one can see quite progressive phases in this therapeutic trajectory inspired by Kernberg's point of view. From a Kohutian perspective, there would be more meaning-making and more empathic reflections by the therapist. For example a Kohutian would say: "I hear at what point you were disappointed by what I said last week. I must have said something that hurt you and that was clumsy of me. Can you tell me what you would have liked me to say?"

In fact, that is what Caroline's therapist is doing up to a certain point. This style of dialogue tends to mobilize affect, while Kernberg's method seems to produce more awareness.

These writers remain essential reading for an accurate clinical approach to narcissistic pathologies. They offer two complementary ways of understanding it. We might perhaps use both methods with persons presenting with self-esteem problems. In addition, there is a case for being attentive in order to see which of the two methods should be used first. Sometimes a long period of simple empathic presence is required in order to discern an area that needs to be isolated and confronted in the Kernbergian sense of the word. In the case of some clients this area can be quickly identified and should be named so that the empathic resonance can be put in place and produce a reparative effect.

Let us imagine for a moment a more Kernbergian exchange when Caroline arrives for her session with the following reproach: "You defended Peter and you didn't know that I was proud of what I'd achieved." The therapist would listen to the reproach, check what was happening for herself the previous week, and ask herself whether there was any truth in the reproach. But she would not say anything to the client. A typical intervention would be: "It's striking to observe that what's happening between us now is like what happened between you and Peter." If the client seems interested, the therapist might add: "Can you see the similarity?" If Caroline does not see it and closes down, the therapist does not pursue it. If she says: "I don't know, what do you mean?", the therapist might carry on: "In one situation or another, two people are sitting face-to-face, trying to understand each other. And in one situation or another they achieve just the opposite."

Basically, in relational therapy, one can only find the right approach by allowing each client's thematic repetition to develop. Only from that basis can one work, carefully and skilfully.

Let us return to the question of idealizing and devaluing transference. If one tries to work through them in the therapeutic dialogue, one often fails, because the devalued therapist who wishes to work through the repetition is perceived as if he is doing it to protect himself and restore himself narcissistically! On the other hand, the idealized therapist will be even more idealized if he wishes to work on the idealizing process, for, in the client's eyes, he will become even more remarkable in his humility! Here is a piece of dialogue to illustrate this:

Therapist: "I am struck by the credit you give me. Working with you, I get the impression that everything I say is right. I'd be surprised if that were true. I don't see myself as someone who never makes a mistake."

Client: [emotional] "No one has ever talked to me so simply and humbly. If only you knew how good that feels! I hope one day that I'll be grounded and have enough integrity to be able to be like that!"

In this type of transference, positive or negative, the therapist's identity is wiped out. He is insignificant, he becomes disposable, a piece of psycho- household equipment with remote control. What is both touching and irritating is that for the client, when he idealizes the therapist he loves him. The idea that this "love" might be a depersonalizing attack is quite foreign to him and it will be a long time before he will be able to assimilate it. And yet, idealizing transference *is an attack*, in the sense that it takes away the therapist's identity. It is as if the client is saying: "Listen, I'm not interested in knowing who you are, I don't care, I need you to be perfect. So listen, don't make a fuss and let yourself be perfect!"

Narcissistic transference can momentarily give one a feeling of greatness, but unless the therapist himself has strong narcissistic issues, the intoxication of narcissistic countertransference does not last. Just as well!

We have stressed two things about repetition. The therapeutic relationship may symbolically represent the couple relationship, the authority relationship, and the parent-child relationship, and within it the client may activate his self-esteem issues. He will set up repetitions around idealization and devaluation, perfectionism, shame, and contempt—around as many phenomena as there are in the therapeutic relationship.

Let us now look at the second R, recognition. How do we work with this? Which approaches contain it and make it useful? What reparation can be achieved through therapy?

In order to repair the thematic similarities in the best way, one divides the client's experience into four experiential fields. Each field has two parts: an external one, what is really happening that can be seen by a reliable other, and an internal aspect, internal resonance, representations that are constructed differently to the events visible in the external field.

What we hope to achieve in the area of recognition is to help the client see his contribution to the hateful impasses, as well as to try and give them a meaning. So let us condense a bit of the dialogue:

Cl: I wanted to have a romantic dinner with Peter and it went wrong and he walked out and slammed the door. In other words, I was looking for a triangle and I got a square!

Th: And now what are you hoping for with me?

Cl: But at least if you hurt me it would be by mistake; not like her (the mother) who did it on purpose.

Th: What happened with her?

Cl: She always took the opposite view to my father and criticised me all the time ...

Later in the conversation:

Th: How's it going now with me?

Cl: You're doing something that I could reproach you for and see as an unfair criticism. I might have started to complain and tried to make you feel guilty, but I don't want to do that any more.

Here we can see the beginning of some reparation as she recognizes how often she "wants this" and "gets that". She agrees that in different fields, with three different people, she experiences the same thing. She is beginning to understand that she is the common denominator. "I am probably playing a part in this!" This understanding is reparative, because recognizing these things gives her a slight feeling of having some power over her own life.

Let us stress that thematic similarities must not become a quest for analogies, for then the therapist would inject his own meanings into the client's life. We just have to decode the similarities, keeping them metaphor- and analogy-free and see them as features that keep cropping up. Caroline's therapist may begin to point them out and to say that, on two occasions at least, the client said she wanted this and got that.

"You wanted a romantic dinner and you had a row; you wanted my praise and we had a row. Now you don't really know what you are getting but your internal experience is that things are fine between us! In your childhood you felt criticised by one person and it sounds from your description that you were indeed criticised".

Finally, the therapist starts to work on the possibility that there are links between these phenomena: desire, criticism, aggression, sulking, guilt, shame, etc. In the end, Caroline may get around to saying: "I may claim that I want good relationships but actually, I still need to do some work around criticism and idealization, around being a perfect person who is looking for the perfect partner".

CHAPTER EIGHT

Issues of eroticism

T he processes of attachment are more or less the same for boys and girls. The issues around narcissism, even if they do present gender-specific content, are relatively similar. What is more, those who have written about these developmental issues have, for the most part, spoken of the infant, or of the child or of the baby. The young "girl" or young "boy" are rarely differentiated. In general the first two developmental issues that we have looked at up to now have been "unisex" or at least pre-differentiated in the area of sexuality.

However, we are now going to enter a very different and well-differentiated universe. This universe of the differentiation of the sexes has become full of social, cultural, and political significance over the last 30 years, which makes research less than straight-forward. It can often be seen that these different perspectives can lead to some confusion between the sender and the receiver when approaching this developmental issue. This confusion tends to cloud the distinction between the field of differences and the field of inequalities. So much so, that the former may be mistaken for the latter. Each one of us has grown up, developed, and discovered our-selves irremediably incarnated in a sexualized body. Our identity, our way of seeing ourselves and the world, depends on the odds of our biological destiny. Even at the extreme limits of empathy of one human being for another, lies this total difference between one sex and the other, this opposite sex that attracts us, that worries us sometimes and that remains quite foreign and strange to us. Our age has not completed its exploration of the relationship between the sexes. It is tempting to disqualify the words of the Other, as soon as they belong to the other camp, but if we do this, we divide ourselves into entities that are unable to engage in dialogue. This would result in a particular epistemology claiming that women do not know how to talk about the sexual development of men and that men, following Freud, must confess to their ignorance of the mystery of feminine sexuality and keep their thoughts to themselves.

In fact, a good deal of the knowledge that we have inherited from certain classical theories of development needs to be considered with circumspection. The possibilities—both clinical and fundamental—that research offers us today, the maturation of the epistemology of the human sciences and the now-accepted connection between the physical and the psychic, all this obliges us to question the often speculative heritage of the great explorers of psychosexual development.

However, there's no question of throwing things out! Through the pages to follow, I will invite the reader to consider classical developmental theories, no longer as fully accomplished and universal enlightenment but, rather, as theories that generate hypotheses of meaning that are partial and singular.

Complexity is inherent in this area of exploration. We are entering a universe where we are must combine temperament and character, representations of Self and the Other, drives and object relations, the body and the mind.

The issues of eroticism last a lifetime, as do the others, but the critical phase at issue here appears above all around three years old if we adhere to the Freudian tradition.

The developmental issue of love and its relationship to sexuality is at the core of the construction of our sexual identity. Our experience of erotic life as infants will later nourish our narcissistic revitalization as sexualized adults. Notwithstanding that biomedical technology now makes it possible to create life without the body to body contact that we have known since the beginning of time, for most people erotic pleasure continues to be the basis of their capacity to become parents. Later the richness of our capacity for erotic love will fortify our resilience in the face of certain developmental crises: aging, menopause, and loss of libido. Throughout the life cycle ultimately, the resolution of the fundamental tension between what is desired and what is forbidden will depend on our sense of the ethical and our capacity to generate life-affirming energy from our passion.

Developmental theories of the development of love and sexuality; or how our aptitude for erotic love is constructed

The developmental theories that, in one way or another, touch on the theme that we are considering here, are as varied in their authors and their approaches as they are in their degree of controversy. The aim of the present chapter is not to make an exhaustive list. I will attempt, rather, to offer a critical review of hypotheses that, while being debateable at certain levels, have all the same stood the tests of time and clinical practice.

We know that early development—let us agree to call it pre-Oedipal—has been studied from two angles in the psychoanalytic tradition: that of object relations and that of drive theory. Between these two competing perspectives, a relative convergence seems to emerge as previously mentioned: that the pre-Oedipal experience of girls and boys is essentially the same.

Where are we today?

Only fairly recently has the body come to occupy a central position in developmental theory—the body and its shape, the body and its specific chemistry, its genetic make-up, hormonal life, and its evolutionary function. In this era where the differences between the sexes are under close examination and we are discovering behind certain differences (held to be natural or universal) cultural reproductions that assure the continuation of matriarchal or patriarchal structures of power, it is useful to remember some of the biological differences between the sexes. These differences have not yet been contested or ironed out. ... From there, we will try to trace the specific developmental agenda of boys and of girls, ridding ourselves as much as possible of cultural baggage that impedes understanding of real differential development.

Firstly, girls experience their prenatal development within a body that is similar to their own, and they are born from this similar body, that of their mother. Boys develop in a body that is different from theirs and are born from a body that is different. In the next stage girls, who have become women, must meet with a body that is different to their own and that of their mother from whom they were born. This body is the "unknown" to them. On their side, boys, in order to procreate, must encounter a body that is different to their own and that of their father and similar to that of the mother from whom they are born: a body that is "known".

Girls have the experience of menstruating from puberty until the menopause. The sign of their ability to conceive a child begins with this monthly loss of blood and often the pain that accompanies it. The rhythm of their life will depend upon this cycle as long as they are of an age to procreate. Boys know that they are reaching the age of manhood and the possibility of inseminating life with the arrival of semen, and therefore genital pleasure. This entry into manhood is not accompanied by pain. There is no bleeding or pain to mark their coming of age. Finally, boys are not destined to carry another life within them, to nourish with their substance another body within their body. Girls can conceive and give birth to a child, which is "naturally" painful.

If we agree that these fundamental biological and physical differences exist, anyone that says that there is no inequality between the sexes may have a different agenda to that of the psychotherapist. Let us leave that to the arena of politics. What remains, then, of the classical developmental theories with their string of controversial propositions around penis envy, castration, and virility? To be honest, we do not really know. These concepts belong to a mode of hypotheses that cannot be verified, which does not mean that they are not useful. They may just as well constitute the unconscious and universal basis of psychic life as belong to a universe of social conditioning. They may also be the reflections of male chauvinists or feminist sexists, handed down and given false credibility by a seductive theory. Whatever one might think of these "epistemological torments", the question that interests us here is that of their possible clinical relevance. Outside the biological differences on which we will base a developmental schema, these unverifiable assumptions can be clinically useful, but only in the framework of an equivocal herme-neutic: in other words within the framework of a co-construction of awareness and meaning relevant to a particular client. Let us agree to establish our reflection from a "particularly prudent epistemo-logical position".

When and how are the phases of love and sexuality constructed and metabolized?

According to drive theories, "anatomy is destiny". It is the funda-mental Freudian contribution that unrelentingly reminds us that individuals have a body and a sex!

And so, according to Freudian theory, the Oedipal situation begins when, between the ages of three and five the child goes through the phallic phase. According to Cournut, the Oedipal situation into which the young child is plunged is fundamentally triangulated. In fact, it is experienced as two interlaced triangles. "There are three people, two have the same sex, the other does not, two are from the same generation, the other not ...." (Cournut, 1997). In one triangle, the sexual, the child has someone similar, the parent of the same sex and someone dissimilar, the parent of the opposite sex. In the other, the generational, it is the child that is dissimilar from the parents, who are a couple. It is within this tension between inclusion and exclusion that the Oedipal scene is played out. In the sexual triangle, fantasies of incest with the parent of the opposite sex appear at the beginning of the process of physical maturation. Within this generational trian-gulation, feelings of jealousy, or even unconscious murderous fanta-sies towards the same sex parent, will progressively emerge.

This is a very general overview of what seems to be a universal and unconscious phenomemon: the Oedipal tragedy. If we accept the validity, or at least the utility of this argument, the Gestalt per-spective can add a dimension that does not appear clearly in the Freudian formulations: the Oedipal situation as a field phenome-non. Let us first remind ourselves of the fundamental assumption of the classical theory of the Self of Perls, Hefferline, and Goodman (1951).

"All human function is an interaction in the field: organism-environment". From the point of view of a relational psychotherapy and its multimodal openness, our reading of the Oedipal situation needs to respect the following parameters:

- The Oedipal situation is an indemonstrable possibility that, from a hermeneutic perspective, can help us make sense of the meaning of an experience.
- The Oedipal situation proposes a plausible explanation of one of the psychophysiological outcomes of development.
- It can only be clinically useful when located in the specific and unique developmental field of the subject.

Without doubt these assertions put considerable limits on the significance of the Freudian contribution and they imply that we need to adjust our reading of the situation. These assertions invite us to respect the uniqueness of each subject in the complex field of the meeting between organism and environment. In considering the Oedipal process, we must reflect on how a client's parents reacted in the Oedipal situation. It is one thing to experience the Oedipal situation with parents that have resolved their own Oedipal issues and a whole different ball game for those whose parents' unresolved Oedipal drama is reactivated.

It appears that there exists a counter-Oedipal situation in the same way that countertransference exists. One could say that how the parents resolved their own Oedipal situation will determine either a developmental risk factor or a resilience factor.

Resolution of the Oedipal conflict for boys

Now that we have established the hypothesis of an Oedipal field, let us look at how, in the Freudian modality, a boy experiences and metabolizes this experience. The first object of love for the male child is the mother. This love of the boy for his mother is experienced as a continuity. The boy does not need to identify a new object of love at the beginning of the Oedipal phase. As a result she who was present as the first object in the development of attachment is transformed progressively and takes on another significance. The boy falls in love with his mother. He wishes to be the centre of her universe, but there is an obstacle: his father. This father, the object that is of the same sex as the boy, but of the same generation as the mother, is transformed in the eyes of the boy. Progressively he takes on the role of a rival. This experience of rivalry can be so intense that Freud went as far as to say that the boy unconsciously fantasizes about killing off this rival.

The father is, for the boy, both an object of love and of identification. But the boy in the Oedipal phase finds himself in a dilemma. And this dilemma manifests itself in relation to the father when he becomes also a threat and a rival. This dilemma, itself a field phenomenon, is internalized by the boy in several different forms, depending on the configuration of the field. However, that which is internalized is likely to be accompanied by guilt and fear of punishment: will the father/rival defend his privileged position with the mother, will he revenge himself, destroy the boy?

According to Freud, retribution means castration. The desire to protect his penis becomes stronger than the sexual desire for mother and the boy renounces her as his object of sexual desire. Freud called this renunciation the "castration complex", and saw it as how the male child resolves the Oedipal situation. Within this scenario, what becomes of the boy's love for father, of the associated feelings of guilt? Because the boy identifies with the father, he decides to find a woman like his mother in order to be like his father. The potentially punitive father is introjected and forms the heart of the super-ego, while the father as a figure of identification nourishes the ideal Self. The metabolizing of the Oedipal situation that we have just outlined is the basis of the Freudian theory that the super-ego develops as the result of the successful resolution of the Oedipal situation. A further subtlety can be added to this: Freud believes that bisexuality is a fundamental aspect of the unconscious. There are, therefore, moments where the boy desires his father and sees his mother as a rival. In brief, in varying degrees according to the field, the love for the father is always accompanied by the desire to kill the rival.

What happens when the boy is not able to resolve the Oedipal dilemma? The dilemma then becomes so polarized and the dynamic tension produced by this polarization so strong that this micro-field is introjected. The relationship with the father contains an intolerable prohibition, even though he remains the indispensable figure of identification. The relationship with the mother is also diametrically polarized. On one side, she represents the indispensable erotic figure, an object of desire. However, the energy of the drive remains in its original state because it has not been synthesized and transformed and correctly attached to pre-Oedipal feelings. The mother, then, equally appears as an intolerable, imprisoning, fused object. The relationship with mother, then, is in itself a dilemma with a very powerful dynamic that necessitates equally powerful defences to keep it out of consciousness. The object of desire is irresistibly attractive but, if the boy is pulled in, he fears he will be trapped forever and regress to more primitive states of dependence.

Resolution of the Oedipal conflict for girls

Freud presumes that girls develop in a similar way to boys. This is what was later called the theory of sexual monism. In fact, in order to remain faithful to the tragedy of Sophocles, we should, like Jung (1913) speak of the Electra rather than the Oedipus complex. Daughter of Agamemnon and Clytemnestra, Electra helped her brother Orestes with the murder of her mother in order to revenge her assassinated father. In contrast to what happens for the little boy, the object of love for the girl is not that of the pre-genital period. The girl child's experience is one of discontinuity. She must leave the maternal object in order to go towards the father. However, as Cyrulnik (1999) writes, the reality of the father is not always obvious. The fragmented father, part genitor, part non-maternal parent, part symbol must be reconstructed and re-presented to the girl child as an object of love. In order for the fragmented father to be available to be integrated, he must, obviously, have resolved his own Oedipal dilemmas, but he must also be "approved of" by the mother as the "right" choice for her daughter. In order to do this she must be able to know him and recognize him in his multi-dimensional and unfragmented identity.

In order for the mother to be able to achieve this synthesis, she must have resolved her own Oedipal issues. If her own erotic issues are resolved, she will know how to recognize and appoint the man-father to her daughter. In order not to disqualify himself in this role of first sexual love for the girl child, to keep the possibility of being a bridge between the pre-Oedipal child and the woman, the father must have reached his own sexual maturity. It is this controlled love that allows him to look at his daughter with a man's eyes, but without desire.

According to Freud, the resolution of the Oedipal situation is achieved through the fear of the possibility of castration. Before rejecting this outright let us take time to listen to what he has to say. We will, then, hold up in contrast some contemporary arguments in opposition to this concept, which today we would consider to be phallocentric.

According to Freud, it is around the age of three that the little girl discovers the existence of the penis. This discovery creates in her a feeling of inferiority, a narcissistic wound that gives rise to the famous "penis envy".

However, systematic observation of young children indicates that boys and girls are conscious of anatomical differences around 16–18 months (Sadock & Sadock, 2000). Outside these empirical observations, several authors, notably De Beauvoir (1949) and Horney (1942), have suggested that these feelings of inferiority or envy that Freud talks about could just as well be attributed to the distribution of power in the field as to the biological characteristics of the two sexes. Why would the boy not be jealous of his mother's breasts or her capacity to have a child, as Adler (1907) had already proposed? The very nature of the feminine genitalia, more interior, less visible, could provoke anxiety without it being linked to the genital apparatus of the boy.

Whatever the case, according to Freud the girl child reproaches her mother for having equipped her less well than males. She therefore turns towards the father as an object of love. The desire to have a child with the father replaces her penis envy. The girl child's discovery of genital inferiority (according to Freud!) can also result in a defiant, hyper masculinity or a neurotic arrest of sexual development. Within this logic, normal femininity implies the renouncing of a "clitoral sexuality". It is obvious today that a theory founded on the genital inferiority of one sex will not attract many followers. Firstly the idea of a little girl reproaching her mother for having equipped her less well than her male counterparts is thoroughly rejected by feminist sociologists, who oppose it with a counter argument. The female child can only be less well endowed than the male if she is born into a society where those that hold the power are men. The reproach of the little girl, therefore, is founded on a political issue not a biological one. She would be more likely to reproach her mother, if there was a reproach to be made, for being submissive to men and for positioning her in submission to men. There is no doubt left today that our knowledge of the subject of sexuality invalidates this theory of genital inferiority. Those who are interested in the classical texts, should read Smith (1991) or Masters and Johnson (1992). For a slightly less classical but no less passionately argued view read Appignanesi and Forrester (1992).

In addition why must the girl child turn to her father following a disappointment? Deutsch (1925, 1944) argued that she turns to the father as an object of love, simply because it is her procreative destiny. Let us go back to the Freudian theory. While castration anxiety generates the resolution of the Oedipal situation for the boy, the fear of losing the mother's love generates the resolution of the Electra complex for the girl. Realizing that her mother disapproves of her desire towards the father, she renounces him in order to maintain the bond with the mother. It is perhaps from this process that we often find that in feminine sexuality the relationship is more important than the drive.

When the girl child does not manage to resolve the Oedipal dilemma, this field phenomenon is internalized and the relationship with the father is experienced as an indispensable link in the development of feminine sexual identity, but equally as intolerable for the development of a social feminine identity. The relationship to the mother is experienced as an indispensable link and a support in the exploration of a masculine universe. However, this link also carries with it an intolerable prohibition of any exploration of the world of the opposite sex.

If we manage to put aside the formulations and the foundations of an argument that is incompatible with our contemporary sensitivity, we notice that these theories are pertinent if they are used within the specific context of hermeneutic dialogue and field theory, exploring hypotheses resulting in an evolving construction of meaning.

What do we observe at adult age when the issue is correctly resolved?

Kernberg (1995) proposes a grid for judging erotic maturity that is very useful in helping the psychotherapist to evaluate the state of the client's developmental issues and to give a certain direction to the therapeutic work.

Firstly, in a healthy adult the full development of oral eroticism and eroticism based on touch is integrated into the libidinal and aggressive drives and this permits a fully developed sexual meeting. We know, for example, that when these drives are not integrated, the erotic meeting is unbalanced. Aggression without libido is only sexual aggression and libido without aggression limits the encounter to the platonic.

In addition Kernberg considers the full integration of genitality in the romantic relationship as a characteristic of adults that are healthy in terms of eroticism. In these adults, eroticism is not limited to the genitalia but also implies all of the pre-genital erogenous zones. Kisses, caresses, and the diverse forms of peri-anal stimulation are part of the range of erotic pleasures.

As for full genital orgasm, it implies involuntary movements that result from a momentary loss of control. In order for this "letting go" to be possible, the person must be capable of a complementary sexual identification, which allows him or her to sense and appreciate the pleasure of the other. This supposes a synthesis of pre-genital tenderness and genital satisfaction. This double genital identification is therefore indispensable for the experience of being in love. It depends on the integration of the homo and hetero sexual derivatives of the pre-Oedipal and Oedipal conflicts. In other words, it is a part of the erotic experience of those who have metabolized the Oedipal phase in such a way as to have retained a positive identification, as much with the same sex parent as the opposite sex parent.

The healthy adult is capable of romantic idealism. This idealism is made possible by a mature engagement towards an ideal that is incarnated and humanized by the love-object. In romantic love, normal idealization relies on the working through of the depressive position (Klein, 1936). This integrates a part of sadness and "grieving" into the idealized, romantic relationship and it is the sign of the establishment of a relationship with a complete object.

The person is hereby capable of reciprocity. As Kernberg writes, "The foundation of eroticism is the capacity to represent oneself as the participant in the orgasm of the other". This supposes a full sexual and empathic identification, founded on erotic "intuition".

What do we observe in adults when the issue is elaborated, but remains unresolved?

For Kernberg, an elaboration of the unresolved erotic issue consti-tutes the fundamental nature of the neurotic structure that can be seen in relatively "high functioning" personality disorders, such as the obsessive compulsive or hystrionic. What characterizes this neu-rotic structure is above all a conflict between desire and the forbid-den. The clinical picture is often marked by experiential impasses where the desire for what is unavailable is manifest yet is at the same time intolerable. At the erotic level, we notice an apparent emotional maturity, associated all the same with powerful genital inhibitions.

What do we notice in adults when the issue is little or not at all elaborated, but a genital capacity is established?

The incapacity to access this developmental phase marks the field of a low-functioning organization. We observe an alternation between "drive without relationship" and "relationship without drive". People like this often have a very strong erotic and orgasmic capac-ity, but can only express it in as much as there is, one can say, no relationship. At the romantic level, one notices a schizoid idealiza-tion based on a splitting of the object.

Let us let some fresh air in—a humanistic look at things: Falling in love and eroticism (Alberoni,1987,1997)

I am not sure if it is Alberoni's translator who is responsible for the expression "enamourment", falling in love, or if it is the author him-self that coined the term.

Let us take the experience of being "enamoured" or falling in love. For Alberoni, this experience of being in love is neither sim-ply erotic nor pleasurable. It consists of a unique and incomparable experience, a radical disturbance of the mind, heart and feelings, which brings together two completely different beings. Falling in love transforms their whole world, it is a sublime experience, an act of folly, but at one and the same moment the discovery of one's own being and one's own destiny. Being in love develops creativity, intelligence, and the capacity to confront real problems in an adult manner. It is a triumph of "*la joie de vivre*" which constitutes a movement towards the desired and projected future. In contrast to the regressive situation, blocked by neurosis, falling in love is liberation, a healing.

Basically, Alberoni considers the adult erotic experience from a teleological point of view, meaning from the point of view of its finality. Field 4 (there and then) prepared the ground for field 3 (contemporary relationships in the here and now) rather than the here and now repeating the there and then.

Alberoni reminds us of this fundamental reality: men and women have always loved each other long before psychoanalysis came and stuck its nose in. Alberoni invites us not to try to reduce either the part of mystery or the impetuous and often irrepressible movement forwards that love generates. He warns us: we must not consider difficult or impossible love as necessarily a symptom of psychopathology. We will look at this further in the chapter devoted to the developmental crises of adult life.

How might it be possible for a psychotherapist to make the "in love" field and erotic experiences accessible to a therapeutic dialogue in a respectful way? There is a simple but proven principle: let us agree to judge this tree (love) by the fruit that it bears (the net result in the person's life). Does this particular love of the patient's generate an infantile regression or liberation? This question should serve us as a guide and help us avoid seeing the work within the narrow angle of normalization. Within this angle, often blinkered, healthy love obviously means two people of the same generation, same power, similar age, each without other attachments. Alberoni reminds us that the heart is an involuntary muscle.

The male and female erotic universes

For Alberoni, pornography belongs to men. He goes so far as to say that it represents the hallucinatory satisfaction of archaic desires and fears that are typically masculine. Bruckner and Finkielkraut (1997) describe the characteristics of the male erotic fantasy as "a series of sexual acts that are not linked by a story and in which the male protagonists have absolutely nothing to do ... man walks around in all innocence and a voracious woman pulls him into her bed" (p. 37).

This pornographic universe is constructed as a marvellous world "where we no longer need to seduce to obtain, where concupiscence will never be repressed or driven back, where the moment of desire is mixed with that of satisfaction, brilliantly ignoring the acting-out face of the other" (p. 37). Effectively, here we seem to have something that resembles the discontinuity in the universe of the erotic development of the little boy that was described in the previous section. This "voracious woman" that pulls the man into her bed is reminiscent of the anxiety generating figure of the pre-Oedipal mother, ready to devour the young male in order to keep him close to her.

Female erotic imagination seems to be undergoing a mutation. In 1987, when Alberoni wrote he could safely say that sentimental novels are a typical manifestation of feminine eroticism in the same way that pornography is for men. However, recent research (Gangestad et al., 2004) has shown that women react sexually to stimuli similar to those that arouse men although they do not show or express their excitement in the same way as men when exposed to the same stimuli.

Today, many pointers lead us to believe that feminine sexuality is less "hidden" than it used to be. One only needs to browse through the women's section of a magazine kiosk to see evidence of this. For example the magazine *Today's Woman* (February 2001) covered topics including "The art of the courtesans", "Lessons in the Kama Sutra", "Tantric sex, does it tempt you?", "101 feminine pleasures", and "10 men pass the test". What are we to think of this cultural shift? There are numerous hypotheses. The topics in today's women's magazines seem to suggest fantasies that are typical of the paranoid/schizoid position, a position to which we are perhaps collectively forced to return. Effectively, socio-cultural norms demand a splitting between one's secret garden and one's public garden.

If this is the case, what can we do in our clinical practice with desire? There is no simple answer!

The developmental issue of erotic love revisited

Biological reality forces us to recognize the developmental differences between girls and boys. Our capacity for love and eroticism implies a synthesis of object relations, of the world of drives, desire, and of the forbidden. Finally the impasse between love and the erotic is just as likely to be a conservative reproduction of a developmental dilemma as a transformational crisis that is itself part of a developmental schema.

Dilemmas of contact in love and eroticism: factors of risk and resilience

Up to now we have been having a look at some psychoanalytic concepts from Freud and Kernberg and we have had a look at Alberoni, an author that we can use as a safety net, stopping us from automatically pathologizing. We have seen the conditions for optimal development according to developmental psychoanalytical theory. We know that these conditions represent a theoretical ideal. We all know people who, without having benefited from ideal conditions, seem to be absolutely fine. Similarly there are those who seem to have grown up in ideal conditions who are not. Therefore the developmental field is extremely complex. No single factor can be determinant. It is multi-factorial.

Let us go back to the risk factors and resilience factors that have already been mentioned. In a multi-factorial developmental field, pathology is the result of a configuration in which the sum of risk factors was greater than the sum of resilience factors.

Let us examine both the self-organism factors and those of the environment.

The organism: factors of risk and resilience

As we have seen in the preceding chapters, we are still in the early stages of understanding when it comes down to temperamental disposition. We believe that certain temperamental configurations might be more at risk than others, but we do not really know much more than that. It does, though, seem that those who are motivated to seek reward and who have a high level of persistence are more resilient than others when faced with a diversity of problems linked to developmental issues.

The family and social environment: 8 risk factors

The following list of factors is the result of research into incestuous families and hysterical presentation. It does not therefore cover the whole of the developmental field. Nevertheless, I have found that an exploration of these risk factors has shown itself to be very useful for work in field 4, particularly when explored within a real hermeneutic dialogue. Effectively, its judicious use allows us to learn more about the configuration of the developmental field of any client.

Risk factor 1: sexual abuse

Mueller and Aniskiewicz (1986) estimate that about 2% of Americans are abused by their biological father before the age of 14. For those who have lived with an adoptive father, the risk is multiplied by seven. According to Finkelhor and Baron (1986), girls are five times more likely to have been abused than boys. Finally, 95% of abused girls and 80% of abused boys have been abused by men.

Risk factor 2: a dissymmetry in parental authority

In some families one parent is dominant, often physically abusive, and another is submissive or withdrawn due either to a physical or emotional "disability", and who is treated as if they are one of the children (Browning & Boatman, 1977; Greene, 1977; Finkelhor, 1979; Herman, 1981). In this configuration, one of the parents represents a supreme authority, which brings the other into the sub-system of the children. Generational boundaries become vague. The dominant parent remains isolated in the parental sub-system, which increases the risk that one of the children will be drawn into the parental sub-system in order to fill the void (Haugaard & Reppucci, 1988, p. 124).

Risk factor 3: physical or psychological absence of the mother

In incestuous families, 33% of the mothers had suffered from a serious illness (Maisch, 1973). In line with this, 50% of women having lived through incest with their father remember that their mother was often hospitalized.

Risk factor 4: role inversion

In certain families, the inversion of roles between mother and daughter is common. The daughter takes on a large part of the role of the mother. The mother wants to be a child and the child wants to be the mother (Justice & Justice, 1979). Several of these mothers are frigid or refuse sexual contact with the father, inviting a reversal of roles.

Risk factor 5: a high level of stress

On the Social Readjustment Scale, incestuous families had an average score of 240, against 124 for non incestuous families. These families had therefore experienced major disturbances or trauma before the incest.

Risk factor 6: a hyper-sexualized family climate

If one of the parents behaves seductively with a child a rivalry is set up between that child and the parent of the same sex for the attention of the seducer. What exactly do we mean by "seducer"? It means attention that is inappropriate, characterized by behaviour where the motivation is clearly sexual, without actually having physical contact or keeping secrets. These behaviours include talking about sex or recounting romantic adventures in front of the child, unnecessary nudity, asking intrusive questions about the child's sexuality, leaving pornographic material in view or buying the child presents, flowers, expensive jewellery, or even underwear, as if she were a lover or a mistress.

Risk factor 7: a puritanical family climate

Inversely, some researchers evaluate very puritanical, authoritarian families as being at risk (Thorman, 1983), as ordinary human sexuality becomes out of bounds.

Risk factor 8: social isolation

Families that are in reality or who keep themselves isolated from the world force the members to turn to each other to get their relational needs met, including erotic needs. Thus clients who grow up in this type of family will be more at risk on the level of erotic development. Isolation not only can reinforce an implacable parental authority, it also leads to an interrupted development of social skills.

The family and social environment: resilience factors

The presence in a family of good and affectionate mentors comes to underpin development and reaffirm the resilience of the child. This may be the effective and affective presence of brothers or sisters, grandparents, or the extended family (Cyrulnik, 2000). In addition, according to Olivier (1994), an early and real involvement of the father in caring for the child's physical needs is a strong antidote to an inappropriate eroticization of the father-child relationship. The father who knows the body of his child from its birth, who holds, changes, and cradles him/her, experiences with the child a continuity that encourages a reciprocal physical maturation in their contact.

In the meeting between the organism (child) and the family (environment), there are two big risk factors. Firstly, a relational field that does not encourage talking things through makes it likely that developmental accidents or risks will not be put into words and available for later discussion (and thereby resolution). This is also a risk in family fields which increases when contact consists largely of silence, censorship, and denial. In addition, a relational field that favours seeing things negatively may increase the risk factor.

On the other hand, there are also two possible resilience factors in this organism-family field. Firstly, a relational field that favours talking about things and an early putting into words of developmental experience constitutes a powerful support for resolution. Secondly, a relational field that favours the recall and discussion of positive elements offers the best conditions (in the meeting between parent and child) for development, with its inevitable hazards, to be talked about and assimilated. This is the case, for example, when the hazards of life are also seen as positive opportunities for development, which inevitably generate a reinforcement of the Self, and the representations of Self through the experience.

CHAPTER NINE

Treating eroticism issues

In order to treat issues around love and sexuality we must first allow a theme to emerge through specific types of impasse that will appear in various experiential fields. Then, meaning must be clinically constructed in order to finally resolve the issue or fully achieve the task at hand. These themes are likely to emerge just as much in fields 1 and 2 as in field 3. As with developmental issues, these impasses are treated and meaning is constructed through cycles of reproduction, recognition, and reparation.

It would, though, be wrong to believe that all impasses in the areas of love and sexuality result from the developmental issues that we have been looking at here. Many people come into therapy because something is not quite right in their romantic relationships but it does not necessarily follow that every romantic impasse is the result of a developmental problem in the area of eroticism. Unresolved issues of attachment and self-esteem are just as likely to undermine the romantic sphere. In other words, pre-Oedipal issues often appear in the romantic sphere and it is important to recognize them for what they are. What particularly characterizes a romantic impasse linked to an unresolved developmental erotic issue is above all a relationship between desire and the forbidden, and other similar bipolar dynamics such as:

- Exhibitionism—voyeurism
- Genitality—orality
- Activity—passivity.

In addition, the therapist must take care to recognize the difference between a relational problem (code V in the DSM) and a personality disorder manifesting itself in the romantic sphere. The therapist must ask himself the question: "Is or will the impasse be essentially the same, regardless of who the partner is?" In other words, does the client carry within him/herself an ability to fully experience *any* romantic relationship? Does he or she have a tendency to sabotage all intimate relationships? If, at the beginning of treatment the relationship seems different from previous ones, the therapist might notice after a while that the client is beginning to experience difficulties similar to those they have experienced in the past? Or, alternatively, the client may seem to flip from one problem to its apparent opposite. Does a client who is not available to be in a relationship have a history of choosing unavailable people? Do they seem to desire only those who do not desire them and vice versa? When speaking of impasses in this domain, this is the basic mechanism to which we are referring.

I will use a clinical vignette with Pierre and a female therapist to illustrate the general idea of the treatment of impasses in the erotic domain.

Pierre: a clinical vignette

Pierre is currently in psychotherapy for the second time. He has been coming for the last four months. He directs a large television production company that specializes in variety programmes. He has been divorced twice and came into therapy with me because he had just left the woman with whom he had been living. He is 50 years old.

He comes from a family of four boys with an absent, alcoholic father and a mother who was inconsistent and egocentric. He felt alone in his family. On the day after his 13th birthday he had to remind his mother about it because she had forgotten. He said that he didn't want to get angry and "crush her with my male power because she was so fragile and diminished ...".

Pierre has made his way in life through sheer determination. He started as a lighting technician, before starting up his own business ten years ago. He is well known and respected in the world of television production.

At 28, the woman with whom he had been living was 22 years his junior. When he met her two years ago he found her interesting intellectually. She had a magnificent body, three children and temporary jobs as a chorister and dancer. She came to live with him. Before long she began to take for granted that everything that belonged to him also belonged to her! Towards the end she wanted him to pay for private schooling for her children and she wanted to stop working in order to "seriously start painting". She said she would support him later on if he wanted to take a year's sabbatical. He refused to meet her demands and ended the relationship. Since then he has oscillated between feelings of having recovered his dignity and depression.

His first wife was a depressive and he had taken care of her for a long time. The second was an unemployed set designer who, he said, had helped him discover art, literature, the finer things in life. Although his most recent partner seemed at first to be highly independent, in time she showed herself to be capricious and controlling. She often told him that he was lucky to live with a beautiful woman like her who was able to teach men how to make love. Pierre thinks that she used him to teach him how to please her sexually. Sometimes she called him "old leftovers".

Pierre believes that he has become hooked on beautiful women and eroticism. Through his work he is in daily contact with ravishing and sexy young women. He has had many adventures but now he wants to find someone with whom he can settle down and with whom he can enjoy a reciprocal love and erotic experience. But he says he is desperate, fears the void, and is afraid that he will never again fall in love.

Cl1:   I've had a good week ... I realise that I've been busy .... I have friends and activities and I'm not doing so badly after all .... On the other hand, in the evening when I'm alone I find that I miss her .... There are times when I would like to go and fetch her, I would tell her just to lie down next to me, not to talk. Perhaps we would make love, a nice moment and then she could leave, still without speaking. Just in order to feel her body next to mine.

Th1:   That body was important to you?

Cl2:   ... She had a beautiful body, firm and sporty and she was proud to show it ... beautiful breasts, sexy bum and she moved them well. Men noticed her in the street, for me that was alright ... I wasn't jealous.

Th2:   Were you proud?

Cl3:   ... Yes, but not overly so.

Th3:   How do you feel telling me about all that, describing her like that?

Cl4:   ... Well, a bit excited and a bit ashamed.

Th4:   ... I can understand what that must be like, to be next to a body that is almost perfect, because you find it beautiful and other men desire it. That is quite something ...

Cl5:   It wasn't absolutely perfect but it was pretty good.

Th5:   There is some pride in your laughter.

C6:   Yes.

Th6:   It must be difficult to let that body go. To make a place for something else?

Cl7:   Ah, it's like I'm going to die. I'm afraid that I'll never fall in love again ... it's like a big emptiness ... there will never again be a beautiful woman ....

Th7:   Why?

C8:   Well, because I rather want somebody of my own age, who will give to me as well ... but it is noble to be the one that gives. And it is also rather exciting to be with somebody who is not ordinary ....

Th8:   There will be other women, but never again this feeling of being with a woman that is extraordinary? Is the physical aspect important ....?

Cl9:   The physical is the most reliable bit. At least that we can see. One can pretend to be kind, good, generous, tolerant, all that .... But it is difficult to pretend to be beautiful. The truth is very quickly discovered. Me, I'm getting older. I meet interesting and generous women of my age but physically it's not quite right ... [Silence ... then] But I pay dearly with the women that I choose ...

Th9:   How?

Cl10:   I accept being the giver, to do the housework, to pay, to shut up, and after all that to receive crumbs in the end ...

Th10:   Do you pretend to be kind ...?

Cl11:   Hmm. Worse, behind all that, I'm full of anger, of sadness ... I feel like I'm old and that I have messed up my life with women .... I would like to have that with someone, make plans with someone, to share .... I don't want to finish my life like I started it.

Th11:   Alone, as in your family, when you were a child?

Cl12:   It was so empty, so dead. I would do anything to get myself out of that ....

Th12:   After that, even crumbs are better than solitude and emptiness .... Better have a capricious and egocentric mother than no mother at all? Despite all, when we talk like that, it seems to me that we are also overlooking something important. It seems to me, that if it was just a matter of you getting yourself adopted, finding yourself an adoptive family, an adopting woman, that is not so hard: you seem to know some warm and generous women that are interested in you ...

Cl13:   That is true. I don't know why it's like that. I have difficulty letting others take care of me. I feel to be the one who takes care of others. It's also a source of pride to be with someone extraordinary.

Th13:   What do you feel when you say that?

Cl14:   I don't know ... I feel a bit ashamed, I find that a bit narcissistic .... It's not really the problem any more, "to have someone" like that. At the same time, I don't want to grow old alone.

Th14:   Perhaps you don't want to grow old?

Cl15:   With her I felt like a desirable young man ....

Th15:   Well ... it seems to me that that is the first time you have said that ... up to now you have mostly spoken about yourself as a desiring man ...

Cl16:   It was that as well, obviously. But I was not ashamed of my desire .... I thought I was up to it ....

Th16:   You know, Pierre, to be attracted to, to be sexually excited or feel aesthetic and erotic pleasure contemplating a beautiful woman, to desire her, is nothing abnormal ...

Cl17:   ... [Emotional].

Th17:   What is happening?

Cl18:   It touches me that you said that to me. You are a woman yourself .... I don't know, you might find me macho ....

Th18:   It seems to me that you have not said that to me very often: you are a woman ... I imagine that it must be a bit difficult for you to speak to me about that, like that ....

Cl19:   That's funny, it's as if I feel a bit uncomfortable. Here I am talking to you about my goddesses and I wonder a bit what that must be like for you. A bit as if I was neglecting you, as if I am ignoring you as a woman ...

Th19:   What might I be feeling there inside?

Cl20:   ...

Th 20:   I could feel as if I'm not good enough ...? Diminished as a woman?

C21:   You are a beautiful woman ....

Th21:   Hmm. Thank you, but I know that I'm, how can I put it, not in the goddess league.

CL22:   It's good what's happening here ...

Th22:   Yes ... . What's going on here?

Cl23:   I'm talking about me, about my desire for women, of my fear of getting old. I am saying it to a woman. To you ... and you are not rejecting me.

Th23:   In that instant there, you are not alone, not in the emptiness ...

Cl24:   I prefer that to the crumbs of goddesses ...

Th24:   [Smiles.] Let's not jump to conclusions too quickly ... crumbs of caviar remain caviar ... and to like that, once again has nothing abnormal about it. But what seems sad, is that for you, without crumbs of caviar, life becomes almost dull and without interest, as if you were going to die. That's what you were saying earlier ...

Cl25:   Yes and no. In fact it is no longer like before. I can, for a long time after our contact or the contact with a friend, not feel the loneliness and the emptiness ... I tolerate being alone much better now. There is no longer only the little boy who is afraid now, there is this part of me, that sees that it makes no sense and who wants to wait to really find a woman, a partner with whom I can share, and who is ready to stay alone for a long while ....

Th25:   I notice that in what you just said to me, you seem to be putting together your therapist and a friend. I wonder if you are not desexualizing a bit what was there a minute ago ...

Cl26:   Perhaps, huh ... and yet I enjoyed that, what was happening between us. And then, on the other hand, it is true that my life is no longer empty, I have friends, projects, my home ...

Th26:   It's true that that part seems more solid ... more filled up. I have an image that your house is no longer empty ... and yet, there is this hole, that gap there where the body of that woman was, there where the body of this woman took you ....

Cl27:   You're not letting me off easily, huh?

Th27:   [Smiles] ...

Cl28:   It is her and the ones before her. You could say that I am still linked with all the women in my life.

Th28:   You say link. I could hear that "I have remained 'attached'" ... and yet I hear more "tied to".

Cl29:   ...

Th29:   What's happening now?

Cl30:   ...

Th30:   I said something that seems to have surprised you ... that got hold of you?

Cl31:   Tied ...

Th31:   Do want to talk to me about it?

Cl32:   [Shakes his head.]

Th32:   Hmm. If we spoke straight away about that, we would be in the secret garden in your body, huh ...?

Cl33:   [Nods his head.]

Th33:   Here, we are touching on your personal sexual universe, your erotic imagination. And I understand that to go there right now would be to go too fast for you. However do I understand that we can bracket this and have a rendez-vous to talk about this in the future?

Cl34:   Yes, I think so. My God, it would be good to talk to you about all that, if I could be sure that I wouldn't disgust you ...

Th34:   [Attentive and friendly silence.]

Cl35:   It's funny, I'm thinking about all the women that I have known ....

Th35:   How are you imagining them?

Cl36:   They are all together in a room sitting down, each one alone at a table for two .... I am the second ...

Th36:   In every sense of the term? ...

Cl37:   Hmm, hmm ...

Th37:   What would you like to do or to say to them when you think of them, now?

Cl38:   I just feel like leaving them and going home.

Th38:   There where ...?

Cl39:   Something else is waiting for me ... my friends, my family; my hobbies are waiting for me.

Th39:   Your life ...?

Cl40:   Yes, and on closing the door, the ties break [smiles]. And I am going to my house where there are tables for six, for three, for four and there is a table for two which is waiting for someone.

Th40:   How do you feel?

Cl41:   Relieved, almost happy. I am thinking of our future rendez-vous. Thank you, Louise.

It is easy to see here that Pierre seems to be as much caught up in attachment and self-esteem issues as in erotic issues. In the framework of the present chapter however, we will limit ourselves to decoding the reproductions that are related to the erotic issue.

Erotic impasses can manifest both in the therapeutic relationship and in the significant relationships of field 3. Obviously the therapeutic relationship is not a romantic relationship in the usual sense of the term, but it is a relationship between a couple! It implies regularity, intimacy, reciprocal attention, and taking risks. When, for example, Pierre's therapist says, "Are you not desexualizing what was happening earlier on?", she is working in field 1. When we work with the themes of love and sexuality, working in field 1 means concerning ourselves with the activation or the resistance to activation of romantic themes, in the here and now of the therapeutic relationship. If the therapist had not intervened in the way that she did it is likely that the theme would never have been brought to light.

She is attentive to catching little bits of thread that might be sticking out and to pulling on them cautiously. In order to improve our capacity to work with a theme that is often underground, clandestine, and full of potential to shame, we must develop the capacity to delicately seize the thread and to pull gently on it without tearing the fabric or undoing the seam.

Field 2 concerns the history of the therapeutic relationship. Sometimes, it is necessary to return to previous sessions where these themes were present, whether they had been named in those terms or not. By saying to Pierre, "This is the first time that you have said: 'You, a woman'", the therapist is evoking the absence of this recognition of her feminine nature up to now in the therapeutic relationship.

Field 3 represents the area that most people go into therapy to deal with. This is the field of significant relationships in the client's present life. In order to work with field 3, it is important to be attentive and to identify the erotic, sentimental, romantic, and even seductive dimensions of the client's present relationships, even those that are not represented in this way. Often clients speak of their current relationships without giving them a romantic, sexual, or erotic connotation. Sometimes they need or hope and yet they fear, that the therapist will question the repressed erotic dimension. That he or he will uncover one way or another what is repressed, deflected, retroflected, or put aside. The principal difficulty of this questioning obviously lies in the need for tact. How is it possible to address the possibility that a professional, therapeutic relationship is erotically charged? In the current climate of complaints and lawsuits against unsuspecting therapists it becomes a very delicate subject to deal with.

By including field 4 in the therapeutic dialogue, we can access that part of the past during which the essential part of these developmental phases that we are talking about took place. It is a case of identifying the phenomenology of significant events of the past and their metabolism in terms of the developmental issues of love and sexuality. One day I said to a woman: "I am struck by the importance that your brother had when you were a young woman. You describe him a bit like a prince charming. You present him to me as your protector who introduced you to the world. You tell me how good-looking he was and that he possessed every positive quality imaginable. Despite the fact that you have always spoken of him as a friend with whom you played, I also imagine that there was a secret love ...." In this intervention I am looking to see if it is possible to add this new dimension to the picture. I am looking to see, with the client, how she might have used a sibling relationship in order to work through the developmental phase of erotic love. Obviously it is easier to open up around relationships with objects that do not have forbidden qualities about them, than those that are forbidden. However, in the developmental past, that which concerns the capacity for erotic love contains objects that are represented as forbidden. Other young boys or girls, the neighbours, uncles, parents, all these become on some level forbidden when we are at the age at which we learn that something of the erotic experience must remain hidden. Alternatively, some clients come into therapy and are already capable of understanding an experience within this context, whether the experience was one of abuse, of seduction, or attraction, or one of erotic or romantic initiation. However, in most cases the past is presented in its non-sexual developmental aspects. It is up to us to discover whether this dimension is present despite being repressed and forgotten.

These clients (when caught up with a crucial and unfinished developmental issue) are also caught up in a series of reproduced events, phenomena, and experiences that are perfect copies of that which remains unresolved. They might, for example, devote their lives to trying to seduce someone inaccessible from a different generation or find themselves in impasses that are less obvious but that continue to carry the same basic structure: the desire for something forbidden. The client will therefore spend his life trying to put in place (and therefore reproduce) this situation in the hope of resolving it. This was somewhat true in Pierre's case.

Reproductions are always rich in meaning. Those that are re-created within the therapeutic relationship have the advantage of being constructed within an environment devoted to decoding and resolving these situations. Our clients reproduce their erotic dilemmas in field 3 and the derivatives of these dilemmas are apparent in the field of the therapeutic relationship. For example: a woman systematically avoids all erotic contact with men and obviously with her therapist, or a man describes a frenzied quest for a sublime mistress which will finally reveal to the world how magnificent he is, and at the same time he denies the erotic capacity of his female therapist or positions himself as a rival with his male therapist.

We can identify these types of reproductions in field 3 through two sorts of experience. On the one hand, we need to consider those experiences that are manifestly erotic or romantic, but on the other hand, we must also pay attention to those other experiences that are apparently of a different type. The most interesting appear and are elaborated in forbidden zones, for example in relationships of authority or in trans-generational relationships and in relationships with people of the same sex. With those experiences that are immediately represented as romantic or erotic or involving longing it is important to ask ourselves if we can hear, in the client's speech, clues that might indicate a reproduction.

When a client speaks of his romantic despair, of the relationship that "didn't work", or another that "seemed to be working", but only because they were ready to compromise, one must listen to all this while holding in mind three questions. Can I hear in this story, something that lends itself to the apparent construction of something forbidden? Is the person putting in place arbitrary types of prohibition or inventing new ones or, alternatively, do they choose situations where the forbidden is already in place? Do I hear, during the client's storytelling, a genital inhibition, meaning by that, a difficulty in totally enjoying the full genital orgasm when it is possible? Finally, do I hear in the discourse, that the erotic or romantic experience is accompanied by a strong denial of affect? These questions act as indicators, thanks to which the therapist can become attentive to what is happening in the romantic relationship, which is a potential site of reproduction of an unresolved issue in the case of eroticism or love.

What did we discover in Pierre's case? It seems that there is some affective denial: on one side we have frustrating goddesses and on the other side warm and welcoming women, "adopting women" as the therapist said, but these ones are not attractive. We therefore have the impression that there is a sort of splitting going on. Do we become aware of the construction of a forbidden object? The therapist is probably perceived to be a forbidden object. If the client is capable of meeting his therapist on a level that includes the sexualized dimension in their contact, he could evolve towards an erotic transference and this transference would be a sign of progress in his capacity to integrate erotic experience in his experience of the object. We should equally continue to work on the relationships in field 3 and their split aspects: the beautiful, desirable women are not "good" and the "good" women are neither beautiful nor desirable. With Pierre the therapist does not insist on doing this work straight away, as she senses that it would be premature. She knows that they need to begin to metabolize the issue. They have a "rendezvous".

These situations in field 3 are always difficult to get to. Pierre, in his willingness to address the issue with his therapist takes us to the heart of the theme. But his ability to bring the issue into the therapeutic field and out of the forbidden zone was supported by his therapist's confirming twice that desire does not need to be justified: a good-looking woman is beautiful! There is an aesthetic and erotic pleasure that does not need any explanation or defence. However, what happens in terms of other experiences, apparently of a different nature, notably in forbidden zones? Here is another scenario in which an erotic issue is brought out of the forbidden zone. Imagine that in therapy a depressed and alcoholic secondary school teacher says: "The only time that I feel good is when I am with my students. They are so alive and full of energy that is so contagious that I feel like I am young again and full of life!" A brave and compassionate therapist who is more concerned with doing a good job than protecting himself might say: "Young people are good looking, they are attractive to look at!" Opening these themes and accessing these experiences does not encourage paedophilia or underage sex but, rather, encourages the client to be able to represent and verbalize the experience.

An important part of the work on the theme of eroticism lies in spotting the erotic or love experience in the therapeutic relationship itself. The expression "erotic transference" is a semantic short cut that hides the shades and textures of an experience that takes many forms. This is a shame because it takes away some of the mystery of this phenomenon and some of its complexity. It is important therefore to try to approach erotic transference phenomena from a more considered and respectful position.

Erotic transference is an aggregate of tender, erotic, and sexual feelings that the client feels towards the therapist. We can, therefore, classify it in the category of positive transference, at least at first sight. A sexual transference that is crude and cut off from delicate and tender feelings is more an incomplete elaboration that has not reached its full development. Gabbard (1994) describes erotic transference as a gold mine hidden underneath a minefield! This is very pertinent. It corresponds to the structure of a relational psychotherapy where to paraphrase Gabbard, we have a series of reproductions that resemble the numerous mines in a minefield and they hide a gold mine: a developmental dilemma that has remained unresolved. An erotic transference is, therefore, a perfect reproduction and we must consider it as the first stage of the reactivation of a developmental process.

Some general considerations on the subject of erotic transference

The majority of studies today focus on the transference situation between a female client and a male therapist. We understand far less the erotic transference of a male client onto his female therapist, and even less the erotic transference of homosexual and transgendered clients. That there exists an erotic transference that a female client has towards her male therapist has come to be seen as rather stereotypical and is easily reduced to something rather simplistic.

Masculine erotic transference

While there has been little research on this type of transference in male clients, there have been some interesting reflections over the last 20 years, notably those of Lester (1985). Accordingly, the therapist who "penetrates" the client's internal universe is in a position that may represent the "phallic" and pre-Oedipal mother. She accumulates revealing observations, tends to induce a regression towards the pre-Oedipal areas, because, from the client's unconscious point of view, she appears as phallic. She is powerful, she reveals what the client did not want to see, she makes him say what he does not want to say, and she makes him feel what he did not want to feel. She is frightening! She is represented more as a pre-Oedipal mother than as an Oedipal object of desire. The more competent the therapist, the less the situation allows the elaboration of an erotic transference because she represents the pre-Oedipal mother and she limits the expression, or even the elaboration of Oedipal desires.

According to Lester this explains why male erotic transference takes a very different path. In addition, the basic position of the boy towards his mother, this pre- and Oedipal object of love and that from which he must tear himself away, will make him see his desire as regressive. For a man, to fall in love with his therapist is to fall back into childhood, to go backwards: it is to want to be rocked and cared for. It is everything except to become a big boy! This representation probably hinders the full elaboration of an erotic transference with the therapist.

Inversely, the basic developmental position of the girl makes her see the therapist as the incarnation of an object of love finally found or to be discovered, which will be experienced as a progressive subjective experience. Women are less anxious in the elaboration of erotic transference because, at first glance and subjectively they may experience it as a developmental experience. "I am going towards ..., I have finally found someone who ...."

Some clients easily accept the regression and the dependence on the pre-Oedipal mother and are less easily accepting of expressing erotic content. They accept the therapeutic experience as long as it is confined to the pre-Oedipal zones and they cannot get out of that zone. Sometimes the shame of their passivity brings the client to reverse the roles and to eroticize the relationship in order to re-establish a dominant phallic position. The client may start to regress, to feel vulnerable. Suddenly he straightens up, pushes out his chest and starts acting proudly in order to readopt a position whereby he becomes the dominating-phallic person and the therapist the admirer. This defence against regression is far more common in men than in women. Erotic transference in men seems in general to be less intense and less persistent than in women. This may be due to a difference in the socialization of the two sexes. In their psychosocial development, women are more encouraged to value connection and continuity, while men are more encouraged to value autonomy. To slide into a regressive link to a pre-Oedipal mother, perhaps appears to them to be against their developmental trajectory.

The erotic transference for men seems to be threatening for their masculinity. Sometimes men will use another woman with whom to enact the erotic transference, thereby not putting in jeopardy their autonomy with the therapist who can then remain a pre-Oedipal mother. The threat is lessened, because the client does not link his erotic desire to this mother. In this case we observe this phenomenon with clients who tell their therapist about a series of erotically charged adventures or misadventures, almost as if the therapist were not a real woman. This seems to be the case for Pierre.

Feminine erotic transference

Feminine erotic transference presents rather interesting contrasts. While men resist eroticizing the therapeutic link, in contrast women tend to eroticize it in order to resist. Obviously at a more abstract level we can speak of all transference as being a resistance. But if we get a little closer to the experience, we see that the erotic transference can be used to avoid talking about something. Some clients elaborate an erotic transference that is so figural that one cannot speak of anything else nor can we speak of the experience of love because the strength of its forbidden nature means that it is too painful. Words are no longer possible.

In those personalities that we call Oedipal, the erotic transference develops slowly and gradually. It is accompanied by embarrassment or shame. The person is unhappy with their experience, which can be summed up like this: "But it doesn't make sense, you are my therapist! What's more I'm not even sure that I'm really in love with you. I find myself thinking about you a lot and that bothers me". These Oedipal personalities recognize the forbidden nature of the relationship: "I know that that's not done, I know I shouldn't and I know that you can't". When it is elaborated in this way, we can imagine that we are engaged in an Oedipal drama.

For the pre-Oedipal personalities, the erotic transference is rather different. Often there is the likelihood of a demand for instant sexual gratification. The person insists, they persist, they cannot see why they should not persist and insist. What they want is the immediate quenching of a desire, whether it be sexual, romantic, or both. Here the internal field and the external field are not well differentiated. Their experience *is* the reality. They may even imagine that their feelings are shared, but that the therapist cannot admit to it because he is trapped by his ethical codes. These people see their desire for the therapist as normal and reasonable: "But it's perfectly normal. These things happen. After all we're human like everyone else?" A client once said to me, "I know perfectly well what you call that. For you it is an erotic transference isn't it? Do you feel better when you call it that?" The ability of these clients to recognize the forbidden and symbolic incest that is contained in the transference is sometimes indicative of an experience in field 4 of seduction and exploitation by a parental figure.

Recognition and the hermeneutic relationship

After these considerations on the nature of reproductions in field 3 at the heart of the therapeutic relationship, let us now look at the principal guidelines for work around recognition and construction of meaning in the erotic transference impasse. It is important to underline the affective competency necessary in order to recognize subtle positive or loving feelings for what they are rather than to reduce all such experience to "erotic transference". This affective competency enables the therapist to be able to make use of both confluence and creative projection for the work in field 3. For example, we can let ourselves flow along with the specific atmosphere that this person carries with them and feel the impact of their seduction, of their sensuality, and of that which impedes their full blossoming. The therapist who has never felt a little twinge of desire for, or even fleeting attraction to a client has probably taken refuge in a theoretical and ethical armour that protects them, but does not allow them much movement.

However, this agreement to risk one's own erotic peace cannot be undertaken without reflexive competence. The therapist that includes him/herself in the field of erotic feelings must do so while being aware and clear about the structure of the phenomena that they decide to plunge into. Informed about the specific types of masculine and feminine transference and the specific universes that go with each of the two sexes, he must take into account the person that is before him and the singularity of reach client's experience. The therapist needs to observe to what extent this client seems to have achieved the synthesis of the genital and pre-genital phases. And finally he must not tar the clinical phenomena with the brush of "erotic transference", just the opposite. He remains open to the non-regressive developmental dimension of the love crisis and of an impossible love.

It is under these conditions that a construction of meaning of the experience becomes not only necessary (as it always is) but possible. The key question for hermeneutic meaning is the following: "What part of the client's story does the reproduction of the impasse contain, whether it is in fields 1, 2 or 3?" Effectively we know that the reproduction of the developmental impasse contains clues as to the sort of meaning that is held in that which remains unresolved or incomplete. Essentially, the types of meaning can be condensed into three dynamics: the impasse as a resistance, the impasse as hostility, and the impasse as a demand for fusion. Additionally we know that the reproductions in field 1 and 2 are linked, on a thematic level, to reproductions in field 3. We could use that which is being elaborated in the therapeutic relationship as a representation of the whole of the client's pathological processes and impasses.

When the greater part of the erotic reproduction in fields 1 and 2 has a flavour of resistance, it is useful to know what preceded the appearance of this resistance. In other words what was it that was relegated to the background at the instant that the erotic transference appeared as a figure? Alternatively, if the reproduction has a more hostile quality, the therapist can initiate the hermeneutic work through their observation of the way the therapy takes on a feeling of being dragged under and the undermining of their "power to heal". From this we can say that underneath the surface features of an erotic-romantic relationship there is a hidden desire to hurt, to shame the therapist, or to destroy the connection. Finally the reproduction that carries a desire for fusion often takes on the form of a projective identification whereby a cold and distant object is in some respects deposited "inside" the therapist. The limits of the therapeutic structure thereby appear insensitive, inhuman, and cruel. Often the base of an erotic desire reveals itself to be a desire for a magical fusion such as that where the therapist "knows everything about me without me having to tell him".

Wherever we are with our affective and reflexive competence, they can only be expressed in the dialogue through our interactive competency. Even if we have the capacity to undertake the risk of the erotic sensitivity of the other destabilizing us, and even if we are able to understand this experience in a different way through our capacity to reframe it, we need to bring some of this consciously thought-out experience into the therapeutic relationship.

Here, more than anywhere else, it is important to put the experience into words, and to do this with tact and clarity. Therapists that are worthy of their profession have a mature relationship with the forbidden and know how to put down limits that are necessary to maintain the therapeutic structure. However, this is not sufficient. These limits must not impede an accurate engagement with this love experience in psychotherapy in the quest for a dignified search for meaning.

The basic question therefore is the following: how can one approach and put this experience into words in a way that holds the therapeutic frame whilst allowing a real immersion in the experience? Nothing is more delicate than this putting into words of an experience where each is aware of their own personal logic and where the body does not automatically behave as it might want to. How can we put the fantasy into words without risking a misunderstanding? One must agree that it is easier to explore the possibility of unexpressed hostility when a client arrives late than to seriously explore a possible erotic fantasy when we receive a box of chocolates or flowers for St Valentine's Day! When we have reason to believe that the theme is activated in the therapeutic relationship, it is preferable to take certain precautions before putting forward this hypothesis.

First, obviously the therapist must examine their own personal experience of and feelings towards the person in front of them. If a therapist only diagnoses an erotic transference in beautiful young people, there is perhaps good reason to question their motives. In addition, one should wait to see if the same thematic links of affinity are produced in situations linked to fields 3 and 4. It is important to see in which way the phenomenon is a reproduction. These are some considerations that argue in favour of a certain restraint in work with the reproductions. On the other hand, if we wait too long, we risk seeing the therapeutic relationship taking on a slightly perverted form whereby the therapist and the client take turns in taking on the role of exhibitionist and voyeur: "You can look but you can't touch!"

Given that in this field of intervention, paying attention to our countertransference reactions is so vital, let us go back to the notion of affective competence and examine some classic countertransferential reactions and some of their implications.

1. *The therapist feels attracted or excited by the client*
First of all it is possible that the client *is* attractive or exciting. The therapist being a sexual being, there is nothing that obliges us to think that all erotic arousal is an indicator of something inappropriate. On the other hand, keeping in mind that in the therapeutic relationship gratification is clinically contraindicated and ethically proscribed, we need to question ourselves if the attraction or excitation persists. The therapist may be the target of a complementary projective identification, becoming a representation of the client's desired/desiring parent of the Oedipal phase. It is also possible that the client may represent an exciting or forbidden object from the therapist's field 4.

   If the therapist continues to ignore the problem or does not treat the experience correctly, he may well make his interventions numerous, penetrating, phallic, and prematurely. Perhaps this is a variant on what Fritz Perls called "mind fucking"?

2. *The therapist greets the erotic declaration coldly and in a detached manner*
Sometimes, while the client is struggling with this troubling experience and is trying to explain it, the therapist may become silent, distant, and less empathic. Often, this contrast is due to the fact that the therapist is awkwardly trying to control erotic countertransference. Unfortunately this clumsy attempt may cause the dialogue to become unduly cold to the point of emptying it of any erotic content.

3. *The therapist feels afraid*
It can also happen that the therapist becomes anxious and acts in such a way that an erotic theme is excluded from the therapeutic dialogue. This premature refusal interrupts the reproduction and the client may start to think of the subjects of sex or desire as inappropriate or disgusting.

4. *The therapist encourages the development of the erotic transfer for personal gratification*
Practising this profession often puts us in the position of being gratified. Recognition, admiration, gratitude are at the very heart of the therapeutic relationship. If the therapist is motivated by an excessive need to be idealized, she may enact her own

reproduction. From the client's point of view, the relationship then takes on a sadistic nature: a desirable and unobtainable object is dangled in front of his nose. It is possible that the therapist is doing to the client something that has been done to him before by a parental figure: seducing without gratifying.

Reparation and the real relationship

No matter how far we are into the work of recognition and making meaning, the resolution of these themes can only really be achieved by deep and sustained work around reparation and a joint effort to find an alternative and new solution.

Reparative work around erotic transference can be divided into three areas. Each area can be summed up in one word: no; thank you; why? Each of these is indispensable to the ability to do reparative work. The "no" must be a reparative declaration. It is the laying down the law, making explicit what has been implicit and forbidden. The therapist needs to be able to say, "I will not abuse you no matter how hard you seduce me".

"Thank you" is a reparative recognition of that part of love that is present in the other's approach. This "thank you", if it is sincere, expresses the pleasure that is inherent in being taken for a desirable object. It says, "I can receive your love and your love is not toxic".

Outside the fact that it is in itself hermeneutic, the "why?" or "for what?" or "towards what?" that the therapist asks expresses a real interest, and is therefore reparative for the meaning of the experience. Together the three aspects constitute the beginning of the developmental experience of renouncing what has been toxic or harmful in the past.

The work around reproductions in field 3 is often spread out over a period of time. The erotic content only appears sporadically in the client's speech. The impasses are familiar, full of energy and meaning, and they also bring their own gratification. Finally they implicate real people, who are themselves also psychically implicated in the structure of the reproductions. The starting point of the reparative action consists of asking ourselves as we listen to the story of the impasses: "What part do I play in the retelling of the experience? Who am I in the reproductive fantasy?" Here the configuration of the sexual identities is important: we do not say the same thing nor in the same way to a therapist of the same sex as we do to a therapist of the opposite sex. When the client is the opposite sex to the therapist, is the therapist represented in the client's mind as a parent of the opposite sex or as a fantasy rival? Is the woman who describes her preliminary sexual experiences to her male therapist in the presence of her asexual father-educator or a sexualized man who is "virtually" jealous of the client's partner or perhaps a bit of both?

In contrast, is the therapist of the same sex as the client a parent, a benign figure of sexual identification, a rival, or one who forbids? These questions are never completely resolved and representations fluctuate with the rhythm of the hermeneutic dialogue. In any case the reparatory link relies on the recognition of the activated representations at each moment of the interaction. Supported by these representations we can finally ask the question that is at the base of the reparative action: taking into account the role of fantasy, what would be the optimal response of an object that is wise, calm, and strong?

The three therapeutic competencies in relation to the problems of love and eroticism

Let us conclude this chapter by coming back to the three strands of therapeutic competency, in order to condense here what is expected in the trilogy: reproduction, recognition, reparation.

Reflexive competency

Fundamental reflexive competency necessitates having thought about the relationship between the clinical, the moral, and the ethical.

We could not work effectively with this intimate and delicate theme without having removed taboos and some current conventions from our clinical knowledge. "Political correctness", persistent preconceived ideas, and conventional indignation are not necessarily synonymous with good mental health. Therapists need to be free thinkers in order not to act as moral police. In this light, what is "normal" sexuality? Whose interests does this normality serve?

We also need to be knowledgeable about the differences between the sexes and about the range of human sexuality and sexual activity, and remain attentive to our own biases in order to ensure that they do not influence the therapy. We need to be able to be comfortable with maintaining uncertainty and support a client's ability to make choices. But we also need to consider the question: How can we know the difference between a "pathological reproduction" and free choice in a range of possibilities? To have a lover, or a mistress, or even to have several, is no more pathological than it is to prefer big brunettes to small blonds, large clean shaven men to delicately built bearded ones, or vice versa! So, where is the problem? What is it that remains unfinished and stops the flowering of creative freedom in the flowering passion of erotic and object love? In order for these questions to nourish our clinical thinking, we need to remain vigilant in situations where an object relation and erotic fulfilment seem to operate on two different levels.

Affective competency

The construction of our affective competency is directly related to the number of personal blocks that we eliminate from the complex set of feelings relating to erotic experience. We should be able to get to the point where we are no longer embarrassed by anything that we think or feel including, paradoxically, shame. In order to advance within this universe where the body has its own logic, we need to be able to accept all of our feelings, thoughts, and our fantasies.

What is more, in order to avoid a type of reductionism in the often turbulent experiences that are love and eroticism, we need to be able to see them fully for what they are: fundamental human experiences, that are sometimes painful, sometimes related to pathololology but that cannot be reduced to this alone.

In order to do this, we must accept and be aware of our relationship to our own sexuality and to our own potential for seduction, regardless of their idiosyncracies, because these are elements of the therapeutic work.

Interactive competency

Finally, all the personal therapeutic work that the preceding considerations presuppose will not be sufficient and effective if we do not know how to place our knowledge and our affective resonance at the heart of the therapeutic interaction. Clients do not approach the theme of sexuality easily. In order to be able to invite them to speak about this, we need courage, tact, and clarity. We need to cultivate the richness and precision of our vocabulary in order to avoid the case where the erotic experience recoils from speech that, while being precise, has a cold and clinical quality about it. In other words we need to be able to draw as much upon the language of the profane as the profound. Finally, in order for therapeutic work around the theme of eroticism to be undertaken in the optimal conditions of resonance, humanity, and security, we must establish limits and maintain the therapeutic frame, while at the same time not limiting either our own or our client's feelings and fantasies and the capacity for verbal exploration.

CHAPTER TEN

Developmental crises in adult life

The psychotherapist's job is to find the roots of his client's suffering by employing active presence, resonance, and empathic listening in order to tune in to a network of signals that lead him to identify the roots of unfinished business. Affective and interactive presence needs to be supported by knowledge and understanding of the developmental past.

But not all suffering can be put down to unfinished developmental business. Development is a life-long process. Sometimes, predictable developmental phases turn into crises without being exact reproductions of unfinished business. What follows is a consideration of development in adulthood and the crises that may occur.

Crises in adulthood are often life's turning points, altering the direction and modulating the experiences of the rest of one's life.

Developmental crises in adulthood are characteristically different from those of early development. Issues of attachment, self-esteem, and eroticism are common to everyone. Of course, not all of us have yet been through every typical adult crisis, but then, we have not finished living yet! Sometimes the client is older than the therapist and is going through crises that the therapist has not yet experienced.

When we are working through early developmental issues, even if the therapist is younger than the client and there is a fundamental empathic understanding, there is less possibility of experiential and emotional mutuality. The therapist must, therefore, possess the right combination of relational qualities and information if he is to help the client.

This next and final chapter is multi-layered. First we will have a look at some of the theories of adult development and the crises that may be experienced during this stage of life. Next, I will suggest some clinical strategies for working with these crises, not only when they reproduce certain developmental themes from the past, but also when they mark something that cannot be regarded as a simple revisiting of past issues. We will move from the past to the here and now realities of growing older. We will also differentiate between developmental crises and the pathological repetition of these crises. Then we will consider the best therapeutic methods to use with our clients, even though we may not have personal experience of the crises that they are going through.

The psychology of adult development

The major theories of early development, which have been central to our training, and still form the basis of theoretical and clinical thinking, were conceived and formulated more than 50 years ago. But the 1950s family was very different to the families of today.

How does early emotional development work in one-parent families, in step-families, in families where there is a great age difference between the parents? Or between the parents and the children? What should we make of the increased involvement of fathers? There are so many unanswered questions, resulting in a less consistent developmental field than that on which the majority of developmental theories are based.

How should we observe and conceptualize the cycle of life at the beginning of the third millennium? Gail Sheehy, a journalist well known for her thoughts on the subject of our "passages" through adult life has pondered this point. First of all, she contends that we take longer to grow up than did previous generations. We know that the concept of adolescence is relatively new; at one time the word did not even exist. Childhood as we know it and as it is represented (a time of innocence, of play, creativity, poetry) is also a relatively recent construct. Working class children used to work on the land, in mines, in factories. In some countries they still do. In middle class and aristocratic families, a child was separated from its mother at birth and handed over to a wet nurse and then a nanny.

The developmental relationships of the human race change and evolve with history, with social and economic conditions, and scientific and cultural advances. Sheehy (1996) makes the point that modern society accepts a lifestyle in which adolescence lasts until the age of 30! It is clear that in certain areas of life (such as access to information, sexuality) 20 year olds are ahead of those of 50 years ago. And yet, they also lag behind them: more of them still live with their parents, unmarried and childless.

If it is true that we grow up later, it must follow that we get old later too! It seems to me that when I was a child in the 1950s, it was rare to see anyone of 50 playing tennis or skiing. Nowadays people play sports and are active when in previous generations they would have been sedentary grandparents.

In our generation there is no real pressure to settle down after the age of 40. "Thirty-somethings" are usually free to explore all manner of things, professionally or in relationships. In the not too distant past, when developmental theories were written, 40 year olds definitely led more settled lives. Unmarried people of 25 were considered "confirmed bachelors" or "spinsters".

Sheehy maintains that each phase of life now happens about ten years later. What happened at 20 now happens at 30; what was expected at 30 now happens at 40, and so on. We need to bear this in mind when we are considering some of the theories of adult development. When we read what some writers propose, we need to ask about the provenance of these ideas.

On the other hand, even though everything has been put back ten years, one phenomenon seems to be going the other way, retirement. Formerly, very few people retired before the age of 65 (or continued working into their eighties because they enjoyed it). Now, 50 is the new 40. It would have been unthinkable a generation ago for people to take early retirement at 55 and go backpacking around the globe. More and more retired people are in good health, very active, pursuing exciting projects. Some even take up a second career. When we look at what different writers say about retirement, we must realize that there is a great difference between choosing to retire at 55 or 65 or even 80.

There has been a big cultural shift in the West since the 1950s. We grow up later, we age later, but we are able to stop work younger. All this will inevitably have a bearing on the type of crises encountered in our therapy rooms and on the questions that will be asked.

Finally, we now have several adult lives. In preceding generations people married once. They had children quite young. These children had grandparents. People had a job or a profession for life. In contrast, many people now train in psychotherapy as a second career. It is not unusual to have children with more than one partner.

Developmental crises in adult life are an increasingly complex modern reality. Some treatment strategies exist to deal with them but the stages are less defined and occur or last often decades longer than those outlined in the theoretical literature on early development. When considering a theory that relates to crises in adulthood one needs to consider when it was written as it matters if it was ten or 40 or 60 years ago.

Relational psychotherapy with reference to adult development

What is the view of relational psychotherapy with regard to developmental crises in adults? This discussion comes from the desire to integrate the theory and practice debated in the previous chapters. We acknowledge the importance of early development. It is obviously indispensable for understanding adult experience. However, we also recognize and wish to integrate the reality and importance of late development, what occurs post six years, post 18 years and so on.

From these "givens" comes an argument that is central to our basic understanding of developmental crises in adulthood. The argument has three conclusions:

1. *The ability to navigate the critical phases of adult development is facilitated, but not determined, by good integration of early developmental issues.*

    If a client has successfully negotiated the three developmental fields, this tends to arm him with the resources necessary for adult development. However, this does not imply that he will always feel on top of the world!

2. *Good integration of early developmental issues does not mean that he will not experience the tensions inherent in the critical phases of adult development.*
The fact that an adult client goes through a critical phase does not necessarily mean an incomplete integration of early developmental issues. The fact of having coped well with early development is an advantage but it does not eradicate the possibility of developmental crises in adult life.

3. *Developmental crises in adult life are likely to reactivate the experience of early developmental issues.*
These three proposals make clear that adult development is helped by successful early development. But it does not eradicate the tensions and pain inherent in developmental crises in adult life. And, integrated or not, developmental crises in adulthood are likely to reactivate the experience of early developmental issues.

Our treatment plan is based on these three points. To say, for instance, that a crisis in adult life reactivates attachment issues does not mean that these issues have not been completed. It simply means that they have re-emerged, and that will be brought to bear on the meaning of the crisis and the direction and possible outcome of the therapy. When addressing a developmental crisis in adulthood, we need to know what we mean by the terms "crisis" and "adult development". The answers are not always straightforward.

What is a crisis?

In medicine, we say that the crisis is the decisive phase of an illness. There is a movement towards either improvement or deterioration. We can speak of a moment of sensory disequilibrium. Thus, a crisis is a sort of sudden loss of balance. What was fine and solid is suddenly disturbed. We do not really know how or if the balance will be restored. Serres (2009) sees a crisis as a transition state between two reparable phases in which a transformation has not occurred, but may yet take place. A crisis places us on the brink of a transformation. We can think of it as a moment of disequilibrium, which may mean a movement towards repetition or transformation. In other words, crisis is potentially the first sign of change. Strange as it may seem, healthy people seem to go through more developmental crises than neurotic people.

It appears that people who are psychologically healthy are more open to thinking of their present equilibrium as a relative and transitory state, a moment on the journey, rather than a final destination. Good mental health implies more openness to new experiences and to change, more courage in the face of the unknown, an increased capacity to question accepted knowledge, and a desire for progress. In contrast to the cyclical and repetitive crises characteristic of low-functioning states, the themes of a developmental crisis in a healthy person are not likely to be repetitions of past ones. The developmental crisis touches on a new theme, which is a preparation for another mode of living.

What is developmental?

Is changing your life partner a development? Or deciding whether or not to have a child? Even psychotherapists would find these questions hard to answer entirely free from value judgements. Seeing a child developing, one has at least some idea what the final product might look like. We can reasonably predict by observing a child the extent to which it will be securely attached, have self-esteem, and be able to love. Predicting the course of an adult's life is less straightforward. What, indeed, does contribute to adult development? According to Erikson (1950), Freud thought that adult mental health involved the capacity "to love and to work". But we also need to take into account questions about the quality as well as the meaning of life when looking at adult development. Let us agree the following: a developmental crisis in adulthood is a time (1) when existing equilibrium is lost, (2) which is accompanied by physical, psychic, or ethical pain, (3) which is accompanied by existential questions, and (4) carries with it the possibility of increased understanding and growth.

A crisis, made up of disequilibrium, pain, and uncertainty, often contains a regressive element of repetition along with a creative, transforming aspect. In this case the client is not presenting a truly developmental crisis. The client may experience something as "missing" but the pain is denied, split off, repressed. He may hide behind a tired, old response to his own questions. In these situations, one of the ways of intervening clinically could be to allow the missing element to come into awareness; to let new questions take the place of old answers. The client will need to feel old pain once more, to let equilibrium be lost where it had been rigidly maintained.

C. G. Jung, Erik Erikson, Daniel Levinson, Roger Gould, Jay Haley, and Charlotte Buhler have all been interested in adult development. Here is a brief précis of their contributions. Following this next section, we will look at the stages of life associated with the developmental tasks of adulthood, likely to restimulate each of the three major developmental issues: attachment, self-esteem, and eroticism.

Carl Gustav Jung

One of the basic disagreements between Jung and Freud was the excessive importance that Freud gave to psychosexual development and to the universal nature of drives. Jung considered psychosexual issues as an important factor in childhood and adolescent development, but he believed that, from adulthood, other realities were more important, notably questions of spirituality and the meaning of life.

Erik Erikson

It has been said that Erik Erikson was the Sigmund Freud of adult life by which we are to understand that he has done as much for the understanding of adult development as Freud did for understanding early development. Erikson's is a general developmental theory covering the whole of life. Erikson suggests stages that are distributed between polarities. We will look at these later. Crises allow reorganization of the personality. In adulthood there are developmental stages that have to be met head on. But a crisis in every one of these periods forces a redefinition and reorganization of our personality traits. This is why it raises anxiety and uses so much energy. Metaphorically, it means deconstructing and rebuilding with the same materials.

Daniel Levinson

Daniel Levinson's model presents adult development as necessitating breaks in stability, leading not to a re-establishment of the old stability but to a new equilibrium. From this point of view, one might say that persistent equilibrium is as problematic as an enduring loss of stability.

His first model (1978) was based on conversations with 40 men from a variety of social backgrounds. Later (1996) he addressed female development.

Although he only presents a small sample, his interviews go deep. What emerges is that personality evolves in six year stages. In the course of these periods, we construct values that make sense to us at this particular stage of life. They are followed by times of questioning and of transition.

Roger Gould

Gould is a contemporary author who suggests seven defined periods around specific themes. These phases have some affinities with Levinson's but appear more focused and precise.

His model is based on observation of a cross-section of a population of middle class, white Americans aged from 16 to 65 years. According to him, an internal clock determines the tasks to be accomplished over seven stages between these years.

Charlotte Buhler

Buhler was a contemporary of Jung. She lived and worked as a psychologist in Vienna in the 1930s. Buhler's theory comes within the humanist-naturalist school. She is a humanist in the sense that she is not a determinist, and a naturalist through the fact that her work is a result of observing her subjects in their natural milieu. Her theory is based on the reading of many personal diaries, particularly those of young people and adolescents. If we agree that these personal writings are more or less faithful records of the questions, crises, pain, hopes, and dreams of their authors, we have a model based on something very rich and very real. Buhler seems to be the precursor of what came to be known in the 1950s as "self-actualization".

She based her theory of adult development around four fundamental "givens" and saw development as an innate drive towards integrating these inborn tendencies. In other words, our existential human destiny, our natural movement consists in integrating them into a harmonious whole. Two propositions are fundamental to us all: we all have a natural tendency to get our needs met and a natural tendency towards egocentricity. But being a social species, we also have a tendency to adjust to our environment by imposing certain limits on ourselves.

Next, we are naturally programmed to express our creativity through professional or personal activities. That is a "given" unaffected by other needs. We need to express ourselves, to encourage the valuing of what is inside us, through meaningful activities.

Finally, we have an innate tendency to maintain and ensure an internal sense of order and balance, while being true to our values. Healthy people develop throughout life trying to integrate these four natural tendencies.

Jay Haley

Jay Haley, one of the pioneers of family therapy, is a prolific writer. His model, including Fleming's 1986 revision, concentrates on the attachment-separation polarity. His view is that developmental stages are essentially cycles of separation and new attachments. These appear as passing phases at different times in life: young adulthood, marriage, parenthood, marital and familial maturity, children leaving home, and retirement.

The six authors described above divide adult life into stages of differing lengths. There is a great difference between some of Gould's four-year stages and the later stages of life described by Erikson that last for a quarter of a century. While those theories that focus on narrow life stages have the advantage of being more precise, in clinical terms they may be more difficult to manage, in the sense that modern life, which is more individualized, more atomized, engenders great individual differences within narrow age limits. And, without ignoring those theoretically useful points proposed for more specific age ranges, it seems more useful for clinicians to work with a less narrowly defined cut-off point. Therefore, I intend to use Erikson's last three stages as well as other writers' theories.

One thing needs to be noted before we embark upon this synthesis: the importance of cultural prejudice, which seems to mark the whole of this area of study. Most of these models and theories seem to refer to a traditional family and linear development, but as we have already seen, life at the dawn of the third millennium is a long way from conforming to this linear model. It should also be added that different developmental theories have to be read with an eye to "the feminine". Indeed, in most theories, heterosexual development and "the masculine" is overemphasized. However, some recent research has included issues particular to female development (Levinson & Levinson, 1996).

According to Erikson, men and women go through the same developmental stages, although women deal differently with the related tasks. For example, they are more interested in intimacy than identity. They think differently from men about a career, seeing it, according to Levinson, more as an insurance than as an end in itself.

In addition, the relationship between work and family is more problematic for women. Women are the "carers" in the home, whether they have a job or not. Thus, 51% of female managers are single, as against 4% of men, and 61% of female managers are childless, as against 4% of men.

Moreover, the thirties are more critical for women, and most have priorities that are the opposite of those they had in their twenties. This is a time for choice and important decisions, since women are impelled by their biological clocks. As a result of nature the realities of middle age hit women earlier than men.

Stage 6: the developmental tasks for young adults of between 19 and 40 years

Tasks that by their nature will reactivate attachment issues

During the first part of these two crucial decades, the young adult must separate from the family of origin. This does not mean a physical separation but crossing a symbolic frontier between two identities. On one side of this frontier, we are, even in adulthood, someone's child. Our roots are in the core of the family and, in times of trouble, this is where we turn for security.

This migration out of the family sphere implies that a young person must distance himself from his parents. This progressive distancing frees up a dose of attachment libido (in the Fairbairnian sense) to be reinvested in a partner or at least in a relatively stable love object. With this love object, who will henceforth be the one we spend most time with, it is possible to become part of a new social network and make new attachments. This attachment movement acts in two ways. Separation from the family of origin frees up an attachment libido that can be invested elsewhere, and the attraction of an adult love object also helps in the distancing from the family of origin.

A new attachment begins in the second part of the young adult's life, if he has children. When children take over part of the attachment libido, the young adult feels less close to his or her partner. The joys and pains and daily routine of having children take up an increasingly major part of the parents' energy. The passion that initially brought them together may weaken or die, however united they may be, and this results in some degree of distress. For some, the respite from marital intimacy may secretly be welcomed, while for others it endangers the emotional safety of the love relationship.

Towards the end of this stage, the young adult is no longer particularly young. The children have grown up. They go to school, have friends, are less demanding and less present. This is a new period of distancing. We have to give up the emotional closeness we had with the children when they were little. At this time the adult is freer and can if he wishes renew and deepen the relationship with his partner.

This stage offers many opportunities to relive the processes of attachment, separation, and individuation. Even in secure people, in the area of attachment, these movements take up a lot of psychic energy. They call into question the nature and quality of relationships and introduce the notion of impermanence. Each of these movements of attachment, of distancing, and of separation may be lived as regressive crises or as progression and development. Mostly, one observes a tension between regression and progression.

Tasks that are likely to reactivate self-esteem issues

The bases of self-esteem need redefining throughout these two decades. Before his twenties, if all has gone well, the adolescent has been trying out his talents, discovering his ideals, if not his precise ambitions. At the beginning of his twenties if he has not already done so he must give up the concept of all-powerful autonomy. He cannot, as before, expect to entertain his friends at his parents' home, nor go wherever he likes in his parents' car! Parental authority carries less weight in his choices. He starts to make his own decisions and to bear the consequences more fully. Sometimes, at this time, the difference between dream and reality means that facts have to be faced. A young man, after considering his options, may come to see that he can not fulfil his dream of going to medical school. And a young woman may finally accept that she has not got the talent to be a professional athlete. Even if, as is very likely, he remains a hero in his parents' eyes, he must now forge his own identity, separate from that of his family of origin. He is not a student; now is the time to find his place in the world socially and materially. He has to make a career, in a socio-professional sphere, in which he will display his talents and receive in return a certain amount of narcissistic gratification. Along with this often come social and psychological pressures to "sort himself out", become "responsible", which does not always feel very heroic!

To summarize, this developmental phase introduces new questions about social roles, of costs, and narcissistic benefits of belonging. The stronger his self-esteem, the better the young adult will be equipped to make good the redefinition of the basis of the esteem that he desires.

The tasks that are likely to reactivate issues of love and eroticism

Even if in the third millennium, young adults have usually had romantic and erotic experiences before the age of 20, it is still the case that, in the time between 20 and 40 years of age, they feel the need, if not to look for a marriage partner, at least to find someone with whom to have a stable relationship. In the course of their encounters, their sexual imagination, their sexual preferences, their feelings about exclusivity or freedom in sexual relationships come up against reality. At the beginning of this stage, sexual libido is at its peak. As they mature, they question, in themselves and also in the Other, the relationship between intimacy and sexuality, of enduring relationship and sexual monotony. They also feel compelled to conform to cultural and commercial stimuli as to what is expected from people of their age and sex. They can often feel bombarded from all sides by erotic stimuli and can find it challenging to steer a steady course. This can be particularly trying as they are also asked to behave in a "civilized" way and be more than just sex objects.

If the early issues of eroticism have been completed, they will be able to integrate their desires and their pleasure into a legitimate and rewarding sexual identity.

Stage 7: developmental tasks for adults of 40 to 65 years

Tasks that are likely to reactivate attachment issues

During this stage—which lasts for a quarter of a century—the adult has to examine the value and the meaning of attachment and of stable relationships. Are they bonds that lead to self-realization or stagnant spaces, a kind of relational warehouse? In fact, the most significant links are already established. It is rare for new relationships that people begin in their fifties, to take root as deeply as old-established ones. The question of relational stability comes up quite often as a reason for going into therapy. Generally, the client does not express the problem in those terms. Mainly, he puts it in a situational context, to do with the partner's character. The therapist who knows about adult development will be doing useful therapeutic work if he asks questions about this. Going into therapy can sometimes be a pretext for looking at these questions of development.

The second developmental task is to stop blaming the other for one's own suffering, one's own limitations, one's own failures. It will be clear in subsequent pages that this prepares the ground for one of the issues of the next stage, the evaluation of one's life.

The third developmental task for this age group is about the entry of children into adolescence and their leaving home. When people speak of the "crisis of adolescence" they are being tautological: adolescence *is in itself* a crisis!

But not everyone agrees. Some writers believe that there is such a thing as crisis- free adolescence. Yes, they agree, there is physical change and a surge in hormone activity, a sort of mutation, but it does not have to be a battlefield. For the mutation of adolescence to be achieved without out-and-out guerrilla warfare, one of the conditions, though not the only one, is that both parents are themselves securely attached. Thus, the adult can participate in the transformation of the adolescent, accepting the ongoing differentiation, honouring his belligerence, and providing for him both a polarity and a model of differentiation. Securely attached parents will keep in mind how difficult it is for the adolescent to separate from someone he really loves and still, really, admires!

Whatever the parents do, the differentiation and affirmation (sometimes oppositional) of the adolescent is going to shake up the relationship. These periods recall early attachment processes which, according to Haley, only make sense to the degree that their polarity, detachment, is also taken into account.

Children leaving home raises once more the question of the bond with the partner. Will it be possible to retrieve it or re-invent it in another, post-parental form? Will the children's leaving signal the start of another phase of attachment with the partner or the acknowledgement that he or she has become a stranger? In fact, stage 7 is the time when it is most likely that one will live among three generations (one's own parents, one's own generation and one's own children). The departure of the children often coincides with the aging and illness of one's own parents. Thus, it is possible to get closer to them, and feel warm towards them. This new closeness raises questions about mourning and forgiveness: mourning for the idealized parents of one's childhood, present mourning in the face of their decline, and mourning to come in the certainty of their death; forgiveness for their past shortcomings, for their gradual weakening, as well as for former misunderstandings. Caring for one's parents is truly living with their limitations, their imperfections, their mortality. This contributes to dissolving possible bitterness and finding the integrity of the Self. We often see this phenomenon in clinical practice: losing one's parents before being able to achieve this rapprochement constitutes a tragic loss from which it is hard to recover.

Attachment issues are virtually certain to be reactivated when the family constellation changes. If early attachment has taken place in favourable conditions, the adult will be equipped to manage this period of redefining significant relationships in his life.

Tasks that are likely to reactivate self-esteem issues

The period between 40 and 65 years is also a time when people realize the need to do or create something to leave behind, to mark their passage through life.

At the start of this stage the polarity of increasing and sometimes exclusive preoccupation with oneself appears. Half one's life is behind one, and, as one advances through this stage the countdown begins. One knows the past, one begins to count the time that is left …. And, with each birthday, the urgency to achieve and leave something behind presses harder. This inevitable time, combined with the children's move towards autonomy, is likely to free up a dose of creative and productive energy, calm and focused maybe, yet anxious and with an awareness that time is running out. In Freudian terms, one might say this is a relative detachment from love objects and a libidinal reinvestment in the Self, a new expansiveness.

One starts to evaluate successes and failures. Previously, the question was: "What shall I do, who shall I be?"; now it is: "What have I done, who am I?" Out of this comes a kind of existential decision, whether to keep going or change course. Whatever the decision, it prepares the ground for another developmental task that appears towards the end of this stage, that of coming to terms with the way one has lived. In the best cases, providing that the early self-esteem issues have been resolved, in or after childhood, one can affirm: "I am naturally imperfect, limited, and worthy, and I can say the same of my life".

Tasks that are likely to reactivate issues of love and eroticism

We have seen earlier in the book, that for many of our contemporaries the question of whether or not to have children often arises in their early forties. During this phase, sexuality is very much linked to the question of procreation. Sexual libido alters with the onset of the female—and possibly male—menopause, and the feeling of a decline in one's ability to attract a partner increases. More than ever, the time has come to confront, to recognize, and to admit one's sexual vulnerability. In the best cases the slow advance of this new vulnerability increases erotic sensitivity and empathy.

When it comes to attraction or physical performance, men and women between 40 and 65 years are up against people who are more beautiful, stronger, more desirable than they. And each knows that time is not on their side. During this 25-year stage, sexual libido changes and overtakes the intimate, personal, immediate act, and moves towards what Erikson calls generativity (1968). This involves taking an interest in society and other people, not just in family members. Erikson believes that the individual does not exist without a family, family not without society, society not without culture, culture not without civilization, and civilization not without individuals. Generativity prolongs eroticism, as Freud (1914, p. 78) writes:

> The individual does actually carry on a twofold existence: one to serve his own purposes and the other, like a link in a chain, which he serves against his will, or at least involuntarily. The individual considers sexuality as one of his ends, whereas from another point of view he is a simple appendage to his procreative plasma, at whose disposal he puts his efforts in return for pleasure, for he is the mortal carrier of a substance which is perhaps immortal, like the inheritor of an entailed property who is only the temporary holder of an estate that survives him (Trans., J. Strachey).

It is in man's awareness of being a sexualized link in the chain of life, which will continue long after he has gone, that the germ of generativity resides. The human being that evolves across this quarter century must become comfortable with the idea of aging and, knowing that he will die, consider his own spiritual evolution, and what he will leave for posterity. The "egoist" libido changes, to a type of love that supersedes the quest for immediate pleasure.

This generativity, which could be seen as a type of generosity, depends largely on cycles of pleasure experienced earlier in life. Towards the end of stage 7, generativity becomes possible, especially if "the mortal carrier of a—possibly—immortal spirit" has been able to enjoy it fully and pass on its meaning to his successors.

Stage 8: developmental tasks for a mature age, after 65 years old

Tasks that are likely to reactivate attachment issues

After the age of 65 there comes a moment where one must break off or progressively dissolve the attachment bonds with one's work and professional identity. In some cases work may have replaced a person. Certain clients speak passionately about their work, almost as if it was a veritable love story, others as though it was a romantic deception. The network of professional relationships that are linked to work will gradually fade away and end with retirement.

We notice that we are now members of the older generation when those who came before us have died and those bonds have disappeared. We are now at the top of the pyramid, one might say at the head of a clan. Sometimes the clan is a little one. Sometimes we can find ourselves alone at the top of this pyramid, contemplating the horizon. We will be among the next to leave.

In the best of worlds, we have an investment in our attachment bonds with the next generation, but often one is caught up in such bitterness towards old age that it is difficult to give to those younger than ourselves. It is as if we have already given too much. When this is the case the end of life is marked by bitterness and one can witness a sort of drying up of attachment.

There is, therefore, a form of solitude that accompanies maturity. The previous generation no longer exists and the following has flown the nest. We see our peers getting older for better or for worse. We see illness and disability befalling those of our age and sometimes we ourselves are fated to be impacted by misfortunes. In the best of worlds, one's partner is still there and the relationship with this person has got deeper with the decades, despite some inevitable fluctuations in the feelings of closeness. In this case, attachment to one's partner increases.

Getting older, illness, and the loss of autonomy mean that aging adults have to be cared for by their children. If they have been able to cultivate a good and healthy relationship, this time of life is perhaps rich in warmth and in connections. However, there is sometimes so much bitterness and rancour accumulated on either side that these connections are bound to fail and old grudges are reactivated.

Developmental tasks that are likely to reactivate self-esteem issues

The final stage of one's lifetime, after 65 years old, involves consolidating one's own personal integrity, in order to be able to look behind and consider one's lifetime achievements with satisfaction. This looking back is the vital condition for a feeling of serenity in the face of one's own death. Not everyone will have realized all of their dreams, accomplished all that they needed to accomplish, and met all the challenges that they wanted to meet. And yet it is this feeling of having done something good, of having made a little difference in the lives of all those that one has known, be it personal or professional, that both quenches and appeases the longing for the ideal.

In the case of the aging adult who sees life as a series of missed opportunities and bad decisions, he or she is bound to absorb and integrate a sense of desperation or failure. The task during this developmental phase, therefore, consists of confronting the last enemies: rage and feelings of injustice before death.

Tasks that may reactivate the developmental issues of love and eroticism

In the realm of Eros, the time has come to accept the decline or the end of the sexual impulse. It is also important to redefine the sense or meaning of our erotic relationships. As the singer Reggiani says, "One must be an artist to the end of one's fingertips in order to sculpt joy when the flesh is sad …."

"Sad flesh" obliges us to revisit our own body image, to love oneself with one's wrinkles. For those whose self-esteem has not developed one single wrinkle of maturity, aging becomes a descent into hell. For others, it is purgatory in the primary sense of the term: a space where one can rid oneself of the remaining elements of physical vanity. When an adult has aged well and accepted getting older, on the erotic level, they can accept aesthetic pleasures and distil subtle pleasures. The wonder of the beauty and the sensuality of things and beings become important.

The body gets older. It no longer obeys as it did before. Physical performance declines and the question is: should one continue with these activities or would it be better to discover new ones? The challenge is how to love this "body-vehicle" that has carried us this far, that tires more easily these days, and that sometimes cannot take us where we want to go?

Finally, the aging of the body and the existential arithmetic which obliges one to count down, forces the aging adult to ask themselves questions about the meaning of death and of their own approaching death. They therefore revisit questions around the meaning of existence itself, as much its joys as its pains, or as Danielle Darrieux, who at 87 interprets Eric Emmanuel Schmitt's *Oscar and the Pink Lady* says, "Happiness is opening the shutters in the morning. But it's closing them in the evening too".

Reproduction or transformation?

"If we do not achieve our developmental destiny, we are condemned to repeating our developmental history" (Ivey, 1986).

How can one distinguish whether a crisis is developmental and therefore facing forwards, towards destiny and a goal, or whether it is, conversely, more pathological: turned backwards towards acting out an unresolved past? Here as elsewhere there are obviously no unique and definitive criteria. However, considering the problem in terms of the polarities of reproduction and transformation can help us better understand the nature of the tension within the crisis and how it is linked to the reactivation of the issues of the past and the movement towards the future.

Table 2 regroups these elements of thinking.

Table 2. Reproduction or transformation?

Familiar risks	*New risks*
Sensation of going backwards	Sensation of going forwards
Presence of unresolved and unrecognized issues linked to the crisis	Absence of unresolved issues linked to the crisis and presence of recognized issues
Clear devitalizing effect	Clear vitalizing effect
Paralyzing affect or insufficient empathy towards the other	Creative empathy towards the other

When a crisis is particularly energized by the repetition polarity, the risks that the client mentions are fairly familiar. The client has often met with these in their life. In the opposite case, when the client's crisis contains the elements of a transformation, the risks to which the client exposes himself have a novelty, a sort of freshness of the unknown. They remain risks, however, with their inherent potential for creating anxiety. We can often recognize the known risk through the client's own words: "If I do this I will gain that, but if I do this I will lose that". In contrast, the client whose crisis involves a greater potential for transformation is often a bit disconcerted by the depths of the crisis. They cannot find the words to express its inherent complexity, because it is new.

In the case of a crisis of repetition, the client seems to be engaged in a backward movement as their experience in field 3 will show. Sometimes, even if they are not fully aware of doing this, they speak about it saying: "Here I am caught up in such and such again! Why does this always happen to me?" In the case of a developmental crisis we touch on the subjective feeling of going forwards, into the unknown and, depending upon the impact of emerging repetition themes, the phenomenon carries the potential for transformation.

At this point an important clarification needs to be made. Sometimes, notably with borderline or narcissistic personalities, the client misunderstands the meaning of the crisis. This may happen to the narcissistic client who has "finally found the ideal partner" and who claims that he or she is now experiencing something completely new. We are not speaking of superficial experience, but something deeper that a correctly calibrated therapeutic dialogue would reveal. For these clients, it is practically a revelation to recognize that in fact they have often "finally found, for the first time in their lives ...". This subjective sentiment is more to be found in the pre-conscious than in conscious experience and it is misleading because it derives from an introjected microfield.

A deeper examination of the critical situation will reveal two phenomena. The first is the presence of unresolved but accessible developmental issues linked to the crisis, or issues as yet unrecognized by the client but accessible to an informed observer. An example might be a young woman who is in love with her teacher who is 25 years older than her. This client experiences, in all her uncertainty, feelings such as those that Jane Bauer describes in her magnificent book *Impossible Love* (2000). If we discover, in her developmental history, a fundamental problem around an absent father and her constant search for needing to be seen by him, she might deny that this has anything to do with it and say that her lover is nothing like her father. In fact it is quite the opposite. This type of denial, that refuses to recognize a thematic link between fields 3 and 4, would tend to indicate that the unresolved developmental issue is infiltrating the present situation. An insistent denial is often an indication of a repetition. In the case of a transformational experience, the therapist will not have identified any historical unresolved issues linked to the present crisis, yet these issues may exist, and be recognized by the client. In this case the young woman might say "It's true that what is happening puts me in contact with whatever happened before. However it doesn't make sense to me to imagine that it is solely due to the past. There may be some truth in that view, but I prefer to stay open to the possibility that, while there is some element of the past, it's more than that".

Here we have the uncertainty and the newness of risk. We may find something in the developmental past that presents the same theme as the current situation, but it would be recognized, taken into account, and used to make sense of the current situation.

The experience of this 25-year-old woman, in love with her 50-year-old teacher who returns this love, is not in itself a desperate situation! However it is possible that the disapproving looks of those around her, including perhaps her own therapist, taint her experience with an Oedipal interpretation and this will be hard to cope with. We are dealing with a crisis whose critical dimension does not come from possible unresolved developmental aspects but rather from environmental pressure.

The net effect of a pathological repetition is devitalization. One can feel that the client's energy is being pulled downwards. We may notice a pattern of whirlwind energy that ends in exhaustion and is ultimately unproductive. Alternatively the net effect of a transformation is one of vitalization. While we may well feel that there is an imbalance, worry, and uncertainty, the client feels full of life.

Finally, in terms of the relationship with the Other, in a pathological crisis we might notice either a paralyzing empathy or a total lack of or insufficient empathy for the Other. In this way the young woman that we just imagined could stop herself acting because of restrictive arguments, such as, "This isn't right. My parents would be horrified to know that I am involved with a man of that age, a married teacher. What about his wife? What about his children?"

I am not saying that she should not take these into account! What is causing the problem is that she is not taking these into account in a reflexive way. She interrupts the complexity of the crisis with an "empathy" that avoids all other considerations, including that of her own experience and that of her love object.

On the other hand, lack of empathy is an indicator of something repetitive being reproduced by the crisis: "It's not my problem. I am living my life; the others can look after themselves". Here we have an absence of consideration for the other and a definite avoidance of the critical dimension of the current experience, an avoidance that will be paid for dearly later on. In both these cases, the crisis is not faced head-on.

There are five criteria which can help the therapist and the client to orient themselves in the inevitable doubt and uncertainty that is provoked by this adult crisis.

Up to now we have defined what we mean by a developmental crisis. We have traced the outlines of the developmental tasks linked to adulthood and the crises that are likely to arise at these stages. Finally we have some pointers that are also likely to help us appreciate the relative impact of transformation and repetition in adulthood. We can now go on to examine some useful general principles for the treatment of the adult crisis, in the context of a psychotherapy that is in its essence developmental.

A general schema of the treatment of developmental crisis in psychotherapy

The treatment of the adult crisis supposes a five axis intervention that can be summarized as follows:

1. Making the connection between the age of the client, their developmental stage and the theme of the crisis.
2. An analysis of the crisis for themes that have to do with:
   • Early and unresolved developmental issues.
   • Elaborating current developmental issues.
3. An evaluation of the tension between the themes of repetition and transformation.
4. A classical intervention approach towards the repetition theme at the heart of the crisis.
5. A hermeneutic approach towards the metamorphosis and potential for developmental transformation that the crisis presents.

It has previously been seen that a hermeneutic dialogue is a co-construction of the meaning of experience. In a dialogical meeting, it cultivates and organizes the contributions that come from the narrative and experiential competence of the client and the affective and reflexive competence of the therapist. Hermeneutic dialogue is the basis for work that is devoted to recognizing pathological repetitions, the ambivalent effort that gives meaning to present experience, renders the universe predictable, and unravels the impasses that are the result of unresolved developmental issues.

As the transformational process is focused on the future, the results cannot be predicted. Working through these changes demands great tolerance of uncertainty on the part of the therapist. This work should be guided by theories covering lifespan developmental stages such as those of Erikson that were referred to earlier on in the chapter.

In the case of repetition the therapeutic work will be largely based on understanding early developmental theories.

The case of Mrs A will help to illustrate the concepts that have been described above.

Mrs A: an illustration

Mrs A is 67 years old. Those close to her, notably her children and a friend, think that she is depressed, that she thinks too much about the past. They are worried about something that might be a sort of monomania. For several years now, she has devoted her time to a subject that her nearest and dearest feel to be morbid.

Mrs A retired two years ago. Her husband died 11 years ago after 35 years of marriage. She thinks that the death of her husband transformed her life and plunged her into something she had carefully avoided up to that point and that she no longer wishes to avoid: her Jewish identity and Jewish history.

Her husband died of cancer while Mrs A was taking a break in the country, at his insistence. She reproaches herself for having listened to him and for nor being with him at the end. It was after this that she became interested in Jewish history, particularly the history of the Second World War and the rise of Nazism. She now participates in all the commemorations, even going abroad. She only reads in order to learn more about this time in history, comparing sources of information and picking up anomalies in the historical facts. Her interest in this subject began after the death of her husband and it has grown considerably since her retirement. She now devotes nearly all her time to it. Her family, who hoped that retirement would be a peaceful time for her, worry when they see her devoting so much time to events that took place 60 years ago. According to them, Mrs A was far better off before she plunged into this sombre universe.

Despite all this, she does have a social life and does not neglect her family life. She looks after her grandson once a week, has friends, and is a member of various Jewish organizations.

In the first interview she appears preoccupied by the missing parts of her story, by the fundamentals of the Jewish religion and by the fact that she has not passed anything on to her children and grandchildren. She does not practise the Jewish faith: neither her Jewish identity nor her religion seemed that important to her until her husband died.

When she was only seven years old, her father, mother, and sister were taken by the Germans and later perished in a Nazi extermination camp. Her grandfather also died later in a Nazi camp.

However, Mrs A had managed to hide and she was reunited with her uncle and aunt who managed to take her to Switzerland. Because they had a child with them, they were not sent back at the border. Her uncle and aunt had severe financial difficulties and she was put into the care of a Jewish family where she was ill-treated and sexually abused. When she speaks of this mistreatment and the sexual abuse Mrs A does not seem particularly affected. She does not deny the serious nature of these events, but it is not this particular part of her history that interests her.

Later she was put into the care of the Swiss Red Cross in Berne who placed her with an elderly Catholic woman with whom she lived for a year and a half. This woman was kind to her and brought her up like her own daughter. Her uncle and aunt however, did not like the fact that young Mrs A was not being brought up in the Jewish faith and decided to take her back to live with them. As they were her closest family they had the right to do this. She therefore lived with them (with an absolute minimum of care) until she was 21.

She studied dental surgery in Switzerland and there she met the man who would later become her husband. He was a Catholic. The couple set up home in the east of France. She had 35 years of happiness with this man whom she describes as not perfect but the man that she needed. She said that he never asked her questions and protected and respected her. She has two children who are married and who are themselves parents.

Mrs A's cognitive processes do not seem to present anomalies. She orients herself well in time and space and her speech is fluent and coherent. Her basic affect seems to alternate between a sort of melancholic sadness and an embodied dynamism, although she does seem to experience a little embarrassment when she speaks of her present subjects of interest. She seems surprised to find herself engaged in psychotherapy. She hopes that it will help her better understand her family and says that she only agreed to consult a therapist to ease their anxiety. At the second session, she said that she doesn't know what to think about her area of interest, which her family feels to be excessive and morbid. She wonders if she might be a bit depressed.

Let us see how we can apply the model in the case of Mrs A.

1. *Establishing the link between the age of the client, her developmental phase, and the theme of the crisis*
At 67 years old, the client is at the beginning of the 8th phase of Erikson's typology. According to these phases it seems that Mrs A has indeed renounced her attachment bond to her work. She is becoming aware that she is now part of the first generation. She is investing in the attachment bonds with the following generation.

In addition it is possible that at the present time she is working on consolidating her personal integrity and that her search for her history and for her community is allowing her to review her life-time. She does not seem to be the victim of despair; she involves herself in her grandson's life and accepts the care that her children give to her. She has discovered an area of vital interest and, in this area, which is one of real identity, she is working through a countdown of her life by seeking to place it in the movement of history. From time to time she sees the woman who looked after her in Berne until she was returned to her aunt and uncle.

2. *Analysis of themes present in the crisis*
What seems to be foremost for Mrs A are the developmental tasks of maturity that are reactivating the major attachment issues and, to a lesser degree, her self-esteem. A therapist might wonder whether there is a relationship between the disappearance of her close relatives and survivor syndrome (why them and not me?) that is playing a role in her current experience. In this case there do not seem to be any indications of resurfacing feelings of guilt or shame. Neither do the traumatic events that followed the family's disappearance, including sexual abuse, seem to play a particular role in the present experience.

As to the question of self-esteem, linked to her identity, she reproaches herself for not having transmitted anything of her Jewish heritage. This said, this self-reproach does not seem to be making her suffer. She seems to be motivated more by a sense of reparation that takes the form of searching for roots, reconstructing memory and being an active witness to her past.

3. *Evaluation of the tension between repetition—and transformation*
Although she seems turned towards the past, we must consider that she is digging into the historical past with a movement towards the future, towards a completion of her identity. Her feelings seem to be linked to what is happening in her life today. She is capable of empathy and understands her relatives' worries. Consequently there is a risk that she will accept and introject their point of view and come to believe that she has a "pathology" that is not clinically observable. The two realities seem to be different. The client is vitalized by her life experience. This vitality does not present clinical signs of any particular form of mania and seems oriented towards a goal and anchored in reality.

4. *A classical intervention around the elements of repetition in the crisis*
Mrs A probably has some emotional residues, introjected micro-fields or other issues that might be useful to explore. Some hermeneutic work that explores possible links between the present and the past (fields 3 and 4) would allow her to make sense of her feelings around her lack of identity and her roots, her need for solidarity, her relationship with her "disappeared" family and those who mistreated her.

However, this work must not aim to complete a past experience that would interrupt the client's ability to undertake present developmental tasks.

5. *Understanding the metamorphosis at the transformation polarity*
The client, if she wanted, could be accompanied by her therapist in an affirmation of the legitimacy of the presenting developmental tasks. She could also be accompanied in an affirmation of her need to look over her life. This would need to be done within a dialogue that is concerned with a construction of meaning around what is occurring now: the sense of the discontinuity that has marked her life and the meaning, as much personal as historical, of her research and her need to be a witness to her history.

CONCLUSION AND EPILOGUE

I wrote this book in order to help my colleagues. I wanted to translate or interpret the various theoretical and clinical material that touches on the increasing focus of the relationship of research to the practice of psychotherapy. I have written about personal and professional matters that are common to us all. In the preceding pages I have suggested that there are three major developmental issues, attachment, self-esteem, and erotic love. I conclude that development continues throughout life, and sometimes appears in the form of crises, which may reactivate early developmental issues. They are the seeds of transformation bringing to the client an awareness of new horizons in his life's journey. Our role is to support our clients in the quest for meaning and understanding that is central to the human experience. I believe that the profession must work hard to meet current challenges. The new scientific knowledge in the areas of affective neuroscience and genetics that is available to demonstrate the complexity of the human psyche also raises more questions than it provides answers. At the same time, and in spite of these new discoveries, psychotherapy has never been under so much pressure to offer short-term results, a paradoxical denial of complexity.

Presented with these changes, psychotherapists must resist oversimplification in our practice. Over and above our day-to-day client work, the good name and value of psychotherapy rests on our maintaining the concept of the uniqueness of each client and his quest for meaning as well as on keeping ourselves up to date with relevant developments in our field and others.

REFERENCES

Adler, A. (1907). *La compensation psychique de l'état d'infériorité des organes.* Paris: Payot, 1956.

Ainsworth, M. D. S., Blehar, M. C., Waters, E. & Wall, S. (1978). *Patterns of Attachment: A Psychological Study of the Strange Situation.* Hillsdale, NJ: Erlbaum.

Ainsworth, M. D. S. & Bowlby, J. (1991). An ethological approach to personality development. *American Psychologist, 46*(4): 333–341.

Alberoni, F. (1987). *L'érotisme.* Paris: Ramsay.

Alberoni, F. (1997). *Je t'aime.* Paris: Plon.

Allport, G. (1937). *Personality. A Psychological Interpretation.* London: Constable.

American Psychiatric Association (1994). *Diagnostic and Statistical Manual of Mental Disorders, Fourth Edition.* Washington, DC: The APA Press.

Apfelbaum, B. (2000). A confusion of tongues: the analytic community. *Journal of the Northern California Society for Psychoanalytic Psychology, VI*(2).

Appignanesi, L. & Forrester, J. (1992). *Freud's Women.* New York: Basic.

Bauer, J. (2000). *L'amour impossible.* Montréal: Le Jour Éditeur.

191

Bayn, N. (1978). *Women's Fiction*. Ithaca, NY: Cornell University Press.

Bellah, R. N., Madsen, R., Sullivan, W. M., Swidler, A. & Tipton, S. M. (1996). *Habits of the Heart: Individualism and Commitment in American Life*. Los Angeles: University of California Press.

Benedek, T. (1958). Parenthood as a developmental phase: a contribution to the libido theory. *Journal of the American Psychoanalytic Association, 7*: 389–417.

Benjamin, L. S. (1996). An interpersonal theory of personality disorders. In: J. F. Clarkin, M. F. Lenzenweger, et al. (Eds.), *Major Theories of Personality Disorder* (pp. 141–220). New York: Guilford Press.

Bensel, R. W. & Paxson, C. L. (1979). Child abuse following early post-partum separation. *Journal of Pediatrics, 90*: 490–491.

Birtchnell, J. (1997). Attachment in an interpersonal context. *British Journal of Medical Psychology, 70*(3): 265–279.

Bollas, C. (1997). The wish of borderline patients. *Zeitschrift Fuer Psycho-analytische Theorie und Praxis, 12*(2): 128–135.

Bouchard, M. -A. & Derome, G. (1987). La Gestalt-thérapie et les autres écoles: complémentarités cliniques et perspectives de développement. In: C. Lecomte & L. -G. Castonguay (Eds.), *Rapprochement et intégration en psychothérapie*. Montréal: Gaétan Morin.

Bouchard, M. -A. & Guérette, L. (1991). Notes sur la composante herméneutique de la psychothérapie. *Revue québécoise de psychologie, 12*: 19–33.

Boutinet, J. -P. (1995). *L'immaturité de la vie adulte*. Paris: PUF.

Boutinet, J. -P. (1995). *Psychologie de la vie adulte*. Paris: PUF.

Bowlby, J. (1958). The nature of the child's tie to his mother. *International Journal of Psychoanalysis, 39*: 350–373.

Bowlby, J. (1960a). Separation anxiety. *International Journal of Psychoanalysis, 41*: 89–113.

Bowlby, J. (1960b). Grief and mourning in infancy and early childhood. *Psychoanalytic Study of the Child, 15*: 9–52.

Bowlby, J. (1969). *Attachment and Loss, vol. 1: Attachment*. London: Hogarth.

Bowlby, J. (1973). *Attachment and Loss, vol. 2: Separation*. London: Hogarth.

Bowlby, J. (1989). The role of attachment in personality development and psychopathology. In: S. I. Greenspan, G. H. Pollock, et al. (Eds.), *The Course of Life, vol. 1: Infancy* (pp. 229–270). Madison, CT: International Universities Press.

Branden, N. (1984). *Honoring the Self*. New York: Bantam.

Brennan, K. A. & Shaver, P. R. (1998). Attachment styles and personality disorders: their connections to each other and to parental divorce, parental death, and perceptions of parental caregiving. *Journal of Personality*, 66(5): 835–878.

Breslau, N., Brown, G. G., DelDotto, S. K., Ezhuthachan, S., Andreski, P. & Hufnagle, K. G. (1996). Psychiatric sequelae of low birth weight at six years of age. *Journal of Abnormal Child Psychology*, 24: 385–400.

Breslau, N., Klein, N. & Allen, L. (1988). Very low birthweight: Behavioural sequelae at nine years of age. *Journal of American Academy of Child and Adolescent Psychiatry*, 27: 605–612.

Bretherton, I. (1992). The origins of attachment theory: John Bowlby and Mary Ainsworth. *Developmental Psychology*, 28(5): 759–775.

Browning, D. & Boatman, B. (1977). Incest: Children at risk. *American Journal of Psychiatry, 134*: 69–72.

Brownmiller, S. (1985). *Feminity*. Columbine, NY: Fawcett.

Bruckner, P. & Finkielkraut, A. (1997). *Le nouveau désordre amoureux*. Paris: Le Seuil.

Buckley, P. (1986). *Essential Papers on Object Relations*. New York: New York University Press.

Bugental, J. F. T. (1987). *The Art of the Therapist*. New York: Norton.

Buhler, C. (1968). *The Course of Human Life*. New York: Springer.

Cassell, D. & Coleman, R. (1995). *Parents with Psychiatric Problems. Assessment of Parenting: Psychiatric and Psychological Contributions.* P. Reder & C. Lucey (Eds.). London: Routledge.

Chevalier, N. & Vandernotte, C. (2000). *Accomplissement de soi et crise du mitan de la vie.* Montréal: Souffle d'or.

Cloninger, C. R. (1988). The genetics and psychobiology of the seven factor model of personality. *Annual Review of Psychiatry, 17*, K. Silk (Ed.). Washington, DC: American Psychiatric Association.

Cloninger, C. R., Przybeck, T. R., Svrakic, D. M. & Wetzel, R. (1994). *The Temperament and Character Inventory. A Guide to Its Development and Use*. St. Louis, MO: Center for Psychobiology of Personality, Washington University.

Cloninger, C. R. & Svrakic, D. M. (1997). Integrative psychobiological approach to psychiatric assessment and treatment. *Psychiatry, 60*: 120.

Cloninger, C. R., Svrakic, D. M. & Przybeck, T. R. (1993). A psychobiological model of temperament and character. *Archives of General Psychiatry, 50*: 975.

Cloninger, C. R., Svrakic, D. M. & Przybeck, T. R. (2000). Personality disorders. In: B. J. Sadock & V. A. Sadock (Eds.), *Kaplan & Sadock's Comprehensive Textbook of Psychiatry, 6th Edition*. London: Lippincott Williams & Wilkins.

Cohn, J. F., Campbell, S. B., Matias, R. & Hopkins, J. (1990). Mother-infant face-to-face interactions of post-partum depressed and non-depressed mothers. *Developmental Psychology, 26*: 15–23.

Commons, M. L. (2002). Introduction: Attaining a new stage. *Journal of Adult Development, 9*(3):155–157.

Cournut, J. (1997). *Epître aux Oedipiens*. Paris: PUF.

Couvreur, C. (2000). *La polarité de l'amour et de la mort*. Paris: PUF.

Cox, S. M., Hopkins, J. & Hans, S. L. (2000). Attachment in preterm infants and their mothers: neonatal risk status and maternal repre-sentations. *Infant Mental Health Journal, 21*: 464–480.

Crittenden, P. M. (1985). Social networks, quality of child-rearing, and child development. *Child Development, 56*: 1299–1313.

Cyrulnik, B. (1997). *Sous le signe du lien*. Paris: Pluriel.

Cyrulnik, B. (1999). *Un merveilleux malheur*. Paris: Odile Jacob.

Cyrulnik, B. (2000). *Les nourritures affectives*. Paris: Odile Jacob.

Cyrulnik, B. (2000). *La vie peut reprendre après un traumatisme*. Con-férence, département de psychiatrie, Hôpital Ste-Justine, Montréal, 4 octobre.

Davidove, D. (1991). Loss of Ego functions, conflict, and resistance. *Gestalt Journal, 14*(2): 27–43.

De Beauvoir, S. (1949). *Le deuxième sexe*. Paris: Gallimard.

DeCasper, A. J. & Fifer, W. P. (1980). Newborn preference for the mater-nal voice: An indication of early attachment. *Southeastern Conference on Human Development*, Alexandria, VA.

De Grace, J. R. & Joshi, P. (1986). *Les crises de la vie adulte*. Montréal: Décarie.

Delisle, G. (1991). *Les troubles de la personnalité : perspective gestaltiste*. Les Éditions du Reflet. Montréal.

Delisle, G. (1992). De la relation clinique à la relation thérapeutique. *Revue québécoise de Gestalt, I*(1): 53–77.

Delisle, G. (1993). La relation thérapeutique tri-modale et l'identification projective. *Revue québécoise de Gestalt, I*(2): 57–86.

Delisle, G. (1998). *La relation d'objet en Gestalt-thérapie*. Montréal: Les Éditions du Reflet.

Deutsch, H. (1925). *Psychanalyse des fonctions sexuelles de la femme*. Paris: PUF.

Deutsch, H. (1944). *La psychologie des femmes*. Paris: PUF.

Dormaar, J., Dijkman, C. I. & de Vries, M. W. (1989). Consensus in patient therapist interactions: A measure of the therapeutic relationship related to outcome. *Netherlands Psychotherapy and Psychosomatics, 51*(2): 69–76.

Dumas, D. (1990). *La sexualité masculine*. Paris: Hachette – "Pluriel".

Eagle, M. (1995). The developmental perspectives of attachment and psychoanalytic theory. In: S. Goldberg, R. Muir, et al. (Eds.), *Attachment Theory: Social, Developmental, and Clinical Perspectives* (pp. 123–150). Hillsdale, NJ: Analytic Press.

Ellis, H. (1977). *Sex and Marriage*. London: Greenwood Press.

Erdelyi, M. H. (1996). *The Recovery of Unconscious Memories: Hyperamnesia and Reminiscence*. Chicago: University of Chicago Press.

Erikson, E. H. (1950). *Childhood and Society*. New York: W. W. Norton, (2nd ed. revised & enlarged, 1963).

Erikson, E. H. (1958). *Young Man Luther*. New York: W. W. Norton.

Erikson, E. H. (1968). *Identity: Youth & Crisis*. New York: W. W. Norton.

Erikson, E. H. (1969). *Ghandi's Truth*. New York: W. W. Norton.

Fairbairn, W. R. D. (1952). *Psychoanalytic Studies of the Personality*. London: Routledge & Kegan Paul.

Faust, B. (1981). *Women, Sex and Pornography*. New York: Penguin.

Fendrich, M., Weissman, M. M. & Warner, V. (1990). Screening for depressive disorder in children and adolescents: validating the Center for Epidemiologic Studies Depression Scale for Children. *American Journal of Epidemiology, 131*: 538–551.

Fernandez-Zoila, A. (1999). *Récits de vie et crises d'existence: une herméneutique métamorphique*. Paris: L'Harmattan.

Finkelhor, D. (1979). *Sexually Victimized Children*. New York: Free Press.

Finkelhor, D. & Baron, L. (1986). High risk children. In: D. Finkelhor (Ed.), *A Sourcebook of Child Sexual Abuse* (pp. 60–88). Newbury Park, CA: Sage.

Fleming, P. (1986). *The Family Life Cycle Model: A Paradigm for Separation and Attachment*. Boston, MA: University of Massachusetts.

Fonagy, P., Target, M., Steele, M., Steele, H., Leigh, T., Levinson, A. & Kennedy, R. (1997). Morality, disruptive behavior, borderline personality disorder, crime and their relationship to security of attachment. In: L. Atkinson, K. J. Zucker, et al. (Eds.), *Attachment and Psychopathology* (pp. 223–274). New York: Guilford Press.

Fontaine, R. (1999). *Manuel de psychologie du vieillissement*. Paris: Dunod.

Franz, C. E. & White, K. M. (1985). Individuation and attachment in personality development: Extending Erikson's theory. *Journal of Personality, 53*(2): 224–256.

French, M. (1978). *Toilettes pour femmes*. Paris: Laffont. Freud, S. (1905). *Trois essais sur une théorie de la sexualité*. Paris: Gallimard, 1987.

Freud, S. (1914). On Narcissism. An Introduction. *S.E., 14*: 67–102. London: Hogarth, 1957.

Freud, S. (1915). Instincts and their vicissitudes. *S.E., 14*: 60–83. London: Hogarth, 1957.

Freud, S. (1920). Beyond the Pleasure Principle. *S.E., 18*: 7–64. London: Hogarth, 1955.

Freud, S. (1921). Group Psychology and the Analysis of the Ego. *S.E., 18*: 65–144. London: Hogarth, 1955.

Freud, S. (1923). The ego and the id. *S.E., 19*: 3–66. London: Hogarth, 1961.

Freud, S. (1931). Female sexuality. *S.E., 21*: 221–243. London. Hogarth, 1968.

Friedman, L. (1988). The clinical popularity of object relations concepts. *Psychoanalytic Quarterly, 57*: 667–691.

Gabbard, G. (1992). Psychodynamic psychiatry in the "decade of the brain". *American Journal of Psychiatry, 149*: 991.

Gabbard, G. O. (1994). *Psychodynamic Psychiatry in Clinical Practice. The DSM IV Edition.* Washington, DC: American Psychoanalytic Press.

Gabbard, G. O. (1997). Psychotherapy of personality disorders. *Journal of Practical Psychiatry and Behavioral Health, 3*: 327.

Gacono, C. B. & Meloy, J. R. (1991). A Rorschach investigation of attachment and anxiety in antisocial personality disorder. *Journal of Nervous & Mental Disease, 179*(9): 546–552.

Galland, O. (1998). *L'entrée des jeunes dans la vie adulte.* Aubervilliers, France: La Documentation Française.

Gangestad, S. W., Simpson, J. A., Cousins, A. J., Garver-Apgar, C. E., Niels-Christensen, P. (2004). Women's preferences for male behavioral displays change across the menstrual cycle. *Psychological Science. 15–3*: 203–207.

Garelli, J. C. (1999). *Controversial aspects of Bowlby's attachment theory.* Buenos Aires Attachment Research Center. (http://www.geocities.com/Athens/Acropolis/3041/)

Gedo, J. E. (1986). *Conceptual Issues in Psychoanalysis: Essays in History and Method.* Hillsdale, NJ: Analytic Press.

Goldberg, S., Muir, R. & Kerr, J. (1995). *Attachment Theory: Social, Developmental, and Clinical Perspectives.* Hillsdale, NJ: Analytic Press.

Gould, R. L. (1978). *Transformations: Growth and Change in Adult Life.* New York: Simon & Schuster.

Greenberg, J. R. & Mitchell, S. A. (1983). *Object Relations in Psychoanalytic Theory.* Cambridge, MA: Harvard University Press.

Greene, N. (1977). A view of family pathology involving child molest – from a juvenile probation perspective. *Juvenile Justice, 13*: 29–34.

Grotstein, J. S. & Rinsley, D. B. (1994). *Fairbairn and the Origins of Object Relations.* New York: Guilford Press.

Gunderson, J. G. & Phillips, K. A. (1998). Personality disorders. In: B. J. Sadock & V. A. Sadock (Eds.), *Kaplan & Sadock's Comprehensive Textbook of Psychiatry, 6th Edition.* London: Lippincott Williams & Wilkins.

Hage, D. (1999). *Attachment Symptoms*. Evergreen, CO: Attachment Center at Evergreen (http://attachmenttherapy.com/ad.html)

Haley, J. (1963). *Strategies of Psychotherapy*. New York: Grune & Stratton.

Haley, J. (1973). *Uncommon Therapy*. New York: W. W. Norton.

Hamilton, V. (1996). *The Analyst's Preconscious*. Hillsdale, NJ: Analytic Press.

Harlow, H. & Suomi, S. J. (1971). Social recovery by isolation-reared monkeys. *Proceedings of the National Academy of Sciences of the United States of America*, 68(7): 1534–1538.

Haugaard, J. & Reppucci, N. (1988). *The Sexual Abuse of Children: A Comprehensive Guide to Current Knowledge and Intervention Strategies*. San Francisco: Jossey-Bass.

Hazan, C. & Shaver, P. R. (1987). Romantic love conceptualized as an attachment process. *Journal of Personality and Social Psychology*, 52: 511–524.

Hazel, H. (1983). *Endless Rapture. Rape Romance and the Female Imagination*. New York: Charles Scribner's Sons.

Heard, D. H. & Lake, B. (1986). The attachment dynamic in adult life. *British Journal of Psychiatry*, 149: 430–438.

Heinicke, C. & Westheimer, I. (1966). *Brief Separations*. New York: International Universities Press.

Henry, W. P., Schacht, T. E. & Strupp, H. H. (1990). Patient and therapist introject, interpersonal process, and differential psychotherapy outcome. *Journal of Consulting and Clinical Psychology*, 58(6): 768–774.

Herman, J. (1981). *Father-daughter Incest*. Cambridge, MA: Harvard University Press.

Holzman, P. S. & Aronson, G. (1992). Psychoanalysis and its neighboring sciences: Paradigms and opportunities. *Journal of the American Psychoanalytic Association*, 40: 63.

Horney, K. (1942). *The Collected Works of Karen Horney (volume II)*. New York: W. W. Norton.

Horton S. L. (2002). Conceptualizing transition: The role of metaphor in describing the experience of change at midlife. *Journal of Adult Development*, 9(4): 277–290.

Houde, R. (1999). *Temps de la vie: développement psychosocial de l'adulte*. Montréal: Gaëtan Morin.

Hycner, R. (1985). An interview with Erving and Miriam Polster. *Gestalt Journal*, 10(2): 27–66.

Ivey, A.E. (1986). *Developmental Therapy*. New York: Josey-Bass.

Jabobsen, T. & Miller, L. J. (1999). Attachment quality in young children of mentally ill mothers. In: *Attachment Disorganization*. New York: Guilford Press.

Jaques, E. (1970). Death and the mid-life crisis. In: *Work, Creativity and Social Justice*. London: Heinemann.

Johansen, K. (1984). Attachment theory in the treatment of hospitalized borderline patients. *Psychiatric Hospital, 15*(3): 113–118.

Johnson, S. M. (1987). *Humanizing the Narcissistic Style*. New York: W. W. Norton.

Johnson, S. M. (1994). *Character Styles*. New York: W. W. Norton.

Jung, C. G. (1933). *Modern Man in Search of a Soul*. New York: Harcourt.

Jung, C. G. (1958). *The Undiscovered Self*. Boston: Little, Brown.

Jung, C. G. (1969). *On the Nature of the Psyche*. Princeton, NJ: Princeton University Press.

Jung, C. G. (1975). *Critique of Psychoanalysis*. Princeton, NJ: Princeton University Press.

Justice, B. & Justice, R. (1979). *The broken taboo*. New York: Mormon Science Press.

Kandel, E. R. (1999). Biology and the future of psychoanalysis: A new intellectual framework for psychiatry revisited. *American Journal of Psychiatry, 4*: 505.

Kantrowitz, J. L. (1986). The role of the patient-analyst "match" in the outcome of psychoanalysis. *Annual of Psychoanalysis, 14*: 273–297.

Kazdin, A. E., Thompson, R. A., Yates, T. T., Marans, S. R., Cohen, D. J., Chess, S. & Thomas, A. (1991). Major general theories of child and adolescent development. In: M. Lewis et al. (Eds.), *Child and Adolescent Psychiatry: A Comprehensive Textbook* (pp. 87–159). Baltimore, MD: Williams & Wilkins.

Kernberg, O. (1974). Mature love: prerequisites and characteristics. *Journal of the American Psychoanalytic Association, 22*: 743–768.

Kernberg, O. (1975). *Borderline Conditions and Pathological Narcissism*. New York: Jason Aronson.

Kernberg, O. (1995). *Love Relations, Normality and Pathology*. London: Yale University Press.

Kernberg, P. F. (1998). Developmental aspects of normal and pathological narcissism. In: E. F. Ronningstam (Ed.), *Disorders of Narcissism: Diagnostic, Clinical, and Empirical Implications* (pp. 103–120). Washington, DC: American Psychiatric Press.

Kissane, D. W. & Ball, J. R. B. (1988). Postnatal depression and psychosis – A mother and baby unit in a general hospital. *Australian & New Zealand Journal of Obstetrics & Gynaecology, 28*: 208–212.

Klein, M. (1936). *Love, Guilt and Reparation. The Writings of Melanie Klein, Volume I*. London: Free Press, 1975.

Klein, M. (1946). Notes on some schizoid mechanisms. *International Journal of Psychoanalysis, 27*: 99–110; *Psychoanalytic Quarterly, 18*: 122.

Klein, M. (1978). *Envie et gratitude*. Paris: Gallimard.

Klein, M. (1994). *Développements de la psychanalyse*. Paris: PUF.

Klein, M. (2001). *L'amour et la haine*. Paris: Payot.

Kohut, H. (1966). Forms and transformations of narcissism. *Journal of the American Psychoanalytic Association, 14*: 243–272.

Kohut, H. (1971). *The Analysis of the Self*. New York: International Universities Press.

Kohut, H. (1991). *Analyse et guérison*. Paris: PUF.

Kohut, H. (1991). *Le Soi*. Paris: PUF.

Koppelman, S. (1976). *Images of Women in Fiction*. Bowling Green, OH: Bowling Green University Popular Press.

Kretschmer, E. (1931). *Physique and Character*. London: Routledge.

Langs, R. (1978). A model of supervision: the patient as unconscious supervisor. In: *Technique in Transition* (pp. 587–625). New York: Jason Aronson.

Leiderman, P. H. & Seashore, M. J. (1975). Mother-infant neonatal separation: some delayed consequences. CIBA Foundation Symposium, *33*: 213–239

Lemaire, P. (1999). *Le Vieillissement Cognitif*. Paris: Presses Universitaires de France.

Lester, E. P. (1985). The female analyst and the erotized transference. *International Journal of Psychoanalysis, 66*: 283–293.

Levinson, D. J. (1978). *The Seasons of a Man's Life*. New York: Random House.

Levinson, D. J. & Levinson, J. D. (1996). *The Seasons of a Woman's Life*. New York: Alfred A. Knopf.

Levy, T. M., Orlans, M. & Winger, S. (1999). *What is Attachment Disorder?* Evergreen, CO: Attachment Center at Evergreen.

Lewin, K. (1951). *Field Theory in Social Science: Selected Theoretical Papers*. New York: Harper & Brothers.

Lichtenberg, J. (1989). *Psychoanalysis and Motivation*. Hillsdale, NJ: Analytic Press.

Liotti, G. (1999). Disorganization of attachment as a model for understanding dissociative pathology. In: *Attachment Disorganization*. New York: Guilford Press.

Livesley, W. J., Schroeder, M. L. & Jackson, D. N. (1990). Dependent personality disorder and attachment problems. *Journal of Personality Disorders, 4*(2): 131–140.

Mahler, M. (1968). *Psychose infantile*. Paris: Éditions Payot.

Mahler, M. (1975). *The Psychological Birth of the Human Infant: Symbiosis and Individuation*. New York: Basic Books.

Main, M. & Hesse, E. (1990). Parents' unresolved traumatic experiences are related to infant disorganized attachment status. In: *Attachment in the Preschool Years*. Chicago: University of Chicago Press.

Maisch, N. (1973). *Incest.* London: André Deutsch.

Makari, G. J. (1997). Dora's hysteria and the maturation of Sigmund Freud's transference theory: A new historical interpretation. *Journal of the American Psychoanalytic Association, 45*: 1061–1096.

Masters, W. H. & Johnson, V. E. (1992). *Sex & Human Loving.* New York: Little, Brown.

McWilliams, N. (1994). *Psychoanalytic Diagnosis: Understanding Personality Structure in the Clinical Process.* New York: Guilford Press. Miller, A. (1991). *Le drame de l'enfant doué.* Paris: PUF.

Miller, A. (1996). *L'avenir du drame de l'enfant doué.* Paris: PUF.

Millet-Bartoli, F. (2002). *La crise du milieu de la vie.* Paris: Odile Jacob.

Millon, T. & Klerman, G. L. (1986). *Contemporary Directions in Psychopathology.* New York: Guilford Press.

Modell, A. (1986). The missing elements in Kohut's cure. *Psychoanalytic Inquiry, 6*(3).

Montuori, E. & Garelli, J. C. (1995). *Outline of the Theory of Attachment. Psychology Notes.* Buenos Aires: Cultural Association for Psychology Research.

Mueller, W. J. & Aniskiewicz, A. S. (1986). *Psychotherapeutic Intervention in Hysterical Disorders.* Northvale, NJ: Jason Aronson.

Muir, R. C. (1995). Transpersonal processes: a bridge between object relations and attachment theory in normal and psychopathological development. *British Journal of Medical Psychology, 68*(3): 243–257.

Mulder, R. & Joyce, P. (1997). Temperament and structure of personality disorder symptoms. *Psychological Medicine, 27*: 99.

Nass, G. D. & Fisher, M. P. (1988). *Sexuality Today.* Sudbury, MA: Jones & Bartlett.

Newton, P. (1995). *Freud: From Youthful Dream to Midlife Crisis.* New York: Guilford Press.

Ochoa, E. (1999). *L'amour au bord de la folie.* Paris: Payot.

Ogden, T. H. (1979). On projective identification. *International Journal of Psycho-Analysis, 60*: 357–373.

Ogden, T. H. (1982). *Projective Identification and Psychotherapeutic Technique.* New York: Jason Aronson.

Olivier, C. (1994). *Les fils d'Oreste.* Paris: Flammarion.

Osborne. C. & Pollack, R. (1977). The effect of two types of erotic literature on physiological and verbal measures. *Journal of Sex Research, 13*(4): 250–256.

Panksepp, J. (1998). Attachment theory, Personality development, and psychotherapy. *Clinical Psychology Review, 8*(6): 611–636.

Perls, F. S. (1969). *In and Out of the Garbage Pail.* Lafayette, CA: Real People Press.

Perls, F. S., Hefferline, R. & Goodman, P. (1951). *Gestalt Therapy: Excitement and growth in the human personality*. New York, NY: Julian.

Peterson, G. H. & Mehl, L. E. (1978). Some determinants of maternal attachment. *American Journal of Psychiatry, 135*: 1169–1173.

Proulx, M. (2002). *Le coeur est un muscle involontaire*. Montréal: Boréal.

Reich, W. (1926). The sources of neurotic anxiety: A contribution to the theory of psycho-analysis. *International Journal of Psychoanalysis, 7*: 381–391.

Reinisch, J. M. & Beasley, R. (1991). *Kinsey Institute New Report on Sex*. New York: St-Martins Press.

Roazen, P. (1992). *Hélène Deutsch, une vie de psychanalyste*. Paris: PUF.

Rogers, C. (1951). *Client-centered Therapy: Its Current Practice, Implications and Theory*. Boston: Houghton-Mifflin.

Rosario, V. A. (2000). *L'irrésistible ascencion du pervers*. Paris: Epel.

Rosenstein, D. S. & Horowitz, H. A. (1993). Attachment, personality, and psychopathology: Relationship as a regulatory context in adolescence. *Adolescent Psychiatry, 19*: 150–176.

Sadock, B. J. & Sadock, V. A. (2000). Normal human sexuality and sexual disorders. In: *Kaplan & Sadock's Comprehensive Textbook of Psychiatry, 7th Edition*. New York: Lippincott Williams & Wilkins.

Schore, A. N. (1994). *Affect Regulation and the Origins of the Self*. New York: W. W. Norton.

Serres, M. (2009). *Le temps des crises*. Paris: Editions du Pommier.

Sheehy, G. (1996). *New Passages*. New York: Ballantine.

Sheldon, A. E. & West, M. (1990). Attachment pathology and low social skills in avoidant personality disorder: An exploratory study. *Canadian Journal of Psychiatry, 35*(7): 596–599.

Sidoun, P. (2000). *Désirs, amours et autres destins noirs*. Montréal: MNH.

Silverman, D. K. (1986). A multi model approach. Looking at clinical data from three theoretical perspectives. *Psychoanalytic Psychology, 3*(2).

Slater C. L. (2003). Generativity versus stagnation: An elaboration of Erikson's adult stage of human development. *Journal of Adult Development, 10*(1): 53–65.

Slobodnik, N. J. (1997). Communication about adoption, personality development and attachment in adoptive families. *Dissertation Abstracts International, Section A: Humanities & Social Sciences, 58*(3-A): 1113.

Smith, T. W. (1991). American sexual behavior: Trends, socio-demographic differences, and risk behavior. *National Opinion Research Center, University of Chicago, GSS Topical Report No. 25*.

Sneddon, J., Kerry, R. J. & Bant, W. P. (1981). The psychiatric mother and baby unit. A three-year study. *Practitioner, 225*: 1295–1300.

Solomon, J. & George, C. (1999). The place of disorganization in attachment theory. In: *Attachment Disorganisation*. New York: Guilford Press.

Solomon, R. F. (1987). *Narcissism and Intimacy*. New York: W. W. Norton.

Spitz, R. A. (1945). Hospitalism–an inquiry into the genesis of psychiatric conditions in early childhood. *Psychoanalytic Study of the Child*, 1: 53–74.

Stern, D. (2000). *Interpersonal World of the Infant: A View from Psychoanalysis and Developmental Psychology*. New York: Basic Books.

Storr, A. (1993). *The Essential Jung*. Princeton, NJ: Princeton University Press.

Sutherland, J. D. (1994). Fairbairn's achievement. In: J. S. Grotstein & D. B. Rinsley. (Eds.), *Fairbairn and the Origins of Object Relations* (pp. 17–33). New York: Guilford Press.

Thorman, G. (1983). *Incestuous Families*. Springfield, IL: Charles C. Thomas.

Tronick, E. & Adamson, L. (1980). *Babies as People: New Findings on Our Social Beginnings*. New York: Collier Books.

Tyson, P. (1994). Theories of female psychology. *Journal of the American Psychoanalytic Association*, 42: 447.

Uddenberg, N. & Englesson, I. (1978). Prognosis of post-partum mental disturbance: A prospective study of primiparous women and their 4-year-old children. *Acta Psychiatrica Scandinavica*, 58: 201–212.

Vaillant, G. E. (1977). *Adaptation to Life*. Boston: Little, Brown.

Vaillant, G. E. (1995). *The Wisdom of the Ego: Sources of Resilience in Adult Life*. Cambridge, MA: Harvard University Press.

Van der Kolk, B. A. (1987). *Psychological Trauma*. Washington, DC: American Psychiatric Press.

Van Ijzendoorn, M. H., Feldbrugge, J. T. T. M., Derks, F. C. H. & de Ruiter, C. (1997). Attachment representations of personality-disordered criminal offenders. *American Journal of Orthopsychiatry*, 67(3): 449–459.

Wakefield, J. C. (1992). Freud and the intentionality of affect. *Psychoanalytic Psychology*, 9: 1.

Waters, E. & Valenzuela, M. (1999). Explaining disorganized attachment: Clues from research on mild-to-moderately undernourished children in Chile. In: *Attachment Disorganization*. New York: Guilford Press.

Waters, P. L. & Cheek, J. M. (1999). Personality development. In: V. J. Derlega, B. A. Winstead, et al. (Eds.), *Personality: Contemporary Theory and Research* (pp. 126–161). Chicago: Nelson-Hall.

Weinberger, D. A. (1998). Defenses, personality structure, and development: Integrating psychodynamic theory into a typological approach to personality. *Journal of Personality, 66*(6): 1061–1080.

West, M. & Keller, A. (1994). Psychotherapy strategies for insecure attachment in personality disorders. In: M. B. Sperling & W. H. Berman (Eds.), *Attachment in Adults: Clinical and Developmental Perspectives* (pp. 313–330). New York: Guilford Press.

West, M., Rose, M. S. & Sheldon-Keller, A. (1995). Interpersonal disorder in schizoid and avoidant personality disorders: An attachment perspective. *Canadian Journal of Psychiatry, 40*(7): 411–414.

West, M. & Sheldon, A. E. (1988). Classification of pathological attachment patterns in adults. *Journal of Personality Disorders, 2*(2): 153–159.

Whiteley, J. S. (1994). Attachment, loss and the space between: Personality disorder in the therapeutic community. *Group Analysis, 27*(4): 359–387.

Williams, D. & Schill, T. (1993). Attachment histories for people with characteristics of self-defeating personality. *Psychological Reports, 73*(3, Pt 2): 1232–1234.

Winnicott, D. W. (1975). *Jeu et réalités.* Paris: Gallimard.

Winnicott, D. W. (1988). *L'enfant et le monde extérieur.* Paris: Payot.

Winnicott, D. W. (1988). *Processus de maturation chez l'enfant.* Paris: Payot.

Winnicott, D. W. (1989). *De la pédiatrie à la psychanalyse.* Paris: Payot.

Winnicott, D. W. (2002). *L'enfant et sa famille: premières relations.* Paris: Payot.

Zazzo, R. (1979). *L'attachement. (2e éd.)* Neuchatel, France: Delachaux et Niestlé.

Zeanah, C. H. & Klitzke, M. (1991) Role reversal and the self-effacing solution: Observations from infant-parent psychotherapy. *Psychiatry, 54*: 346–357.

INDEX

reactivate developmental issues
180–181
reactivate issues 174, 177–178

Mahler, Margaret 37–39
masculine erotic transference
151–153
masochism 9
mother-baby
adjustment 35
couple 35
dyad 33, 35
mother-child
matrix 35
relationship 30
Matrix of Field Representations
(MFR) 14–17, 77, 79
reinforcement of
representations in 17
Miller, A. 95–96, 98–99
Modell, Arthur 106
multi-axial system 1

narcissism 92
concepts of 90
developmental failure
particular to 95–96
healthy 93
in psychology 92
pathological 93
problem of 90
narcissistic
client 112
depression, experience of 101
exploitation, sensitive to 96
False Self 66
needs, amalgam of 97
pathogenesis 112
personality 7, 90
perversion 94
response 113

sensibility 90
transference 117
narcissistic issues
clinical manifestations linked
to 91–92
Nazism 185–186
negative transference 104
Neil, A. S. 98
neurological functions 67
neuro-physiological maturation 38
new risks 181
non-pathological relationship 45
non-regressive developmental
dimension 154
non-verbal sensitivity, powerful 97

object constancy phase 39
object relations development
theories 25
object relations Gestalt therapy
(ORGT) 11–15, 18, 23
personality disorder 13
shares 22
theoretical basis 12
therapeutic process of 18
object-seeking 40
libido 93
Oedipal
dilemmas 128
dynamic 23
interpretation 183
issues 128
process 126
scene 125
tragedy 125
Oedipal conflict
for boys 126
for girls 128
Oedipal situation 28, 125–127,
129–130
resolution of 129–130